TRUST IN EDUCATION
Truths and Values

Discourse Power Resistance Volume 8

Trust in Education
Truths and Values

edited by Jerome Satterthwaite,
Heather Piper, Pat Sikes
and Simon Webster

Trentham Books
Stoke on Trent, UK and Sterling, USA

Trentham Books Limited

Westview House	22883 Quicksilver Drive
734 London Road	Sterling
Oakhill	VA 20166-2012
Stoke on Trent	USA
Staffordshire	
England ST4 5NP	

First published 2011

British Library Cataloguing-in-Publication Data
A catalogue record for this book is available from the
British Library

ISBN 978-1-85856-488-3

Designed and typeset by Trentham Books Ltd, Chester
Printed and bound in Great Britain by 4edge Limited, Hockley

Contents

The Discourse Power Resistance Series: a Reflection

ELIZABETH ATKINSON

The *Discourse Power Resistance* series offers radical new perspectives on educational research, theory, policy and practice for all those in education – students, teachers, trainers, lecturers, researchers, managers and policy makers – who are caught up in the contemporary matrix of globalised, marketised, neo-liberal education and its corrollaries: centralised educational control, external and internal policing by policy makers, managers and co-practitioners and the demands of the audit-and-output society.

In my introduction to the third volume in this series, *Educational Counter-Cultures: Confrontations, images, vision* (2004), I wrote 'This book is a song of resistance.' This description speaks for the whole DPR series. These books, which arise from the international *Discourse Power Resistance* conferences, take key themes out into the educational world: the books, the conferences and the debate they have engendered have generated an academic and political movement which reaches beyond the boundaries of nations and disciplines, bringing together powerful voices from around the world in resistance to the marketised control and ideological policing of education.

These voices include some of the most esteemed researchers in their fields, but the book series is also about letting subaltern voices be heard: through the words of contributors from many nations, new insights are offered from those who are normally marginalised, silenced and powerless. A key feature of these voices is that they are multiple, separate and sometimes dissonant: DPR does not promote single, easy solutions, but offers a kaleidoscope of perspectives on things as they are; and a host of new imaginaries for things as they might be.

DPR has developed an increasingly strong presence in the international research community since its first conference in 2002, and now encompasses at its core a collaboration between the original DPR team at the University of Plymouth, the International Association of Qualitative Inquiry led by Norman Denzin at the University of Illinois at Urbana-Champaign, together with colleagues from around the UK, as well as in the Caribbean, South Africa, Australia and Poland. It has provided a crucial forum for radical critique of contemporary trends in education, maintaining a steady interrogation of the comfort zone of the educational establishment in the light of increasingly draconian control of educational research and practice. Both the conferences and the book series demonstrate the power of research as a subversive activity, research as a way of speaking truth to power (to echo the themes of two recent conferences), maintaining that essential role of the researcher as an independent voice of critique at a time when we are all too easily drawn into regimes of control and practices of compliance.

Other titles in the series

Satterthwaite, J, Atkinson, E and Gale, K (eds) (2003) *Discourse, Power, Resistance: Challenging the Rhetoric of Contemporary Education.* Stoke-on-Trent: Trentham

Satterthwaite, J, Atkinson, E and Martin, M (eds) (2004) *The Disciplining of Education: New Languages of Power and Resistance.* Stoke-on-Trent: Trentham

Satterthwaite, J, Atkinson, E and Martin, W (eds) (2004) *Educational Counter-Cultures: Confrontations, Images, Vision.* Stoke-on-Trent: Trentham

Satterthwaite, J and Atkinson, E (eds) (2005) *Discourses of Education in the Age of New Imperialism.* Stoke-on-Trent: Trentham

Satterthwaite, J, Martin, W and Roberts, L (eds) (2006) *Discourse, Resistance and Identity Formation.* Stoke-on-Trent: Trentham

Satterthwaite, J, Watts, M and Piper, H (eds) (2008) *Talking Truth, Confronting Power.* Stoke-on-Trent: Trentham

Satterthwaite, J, Piper, H and Sikes, P (eds) (2009) *Power in the Academy.* Stoke-on-Trent: Trentham

Introduction

HEATHER PIPER, PAT SIKES, JEROME SATTERTHWAITE
AND SIMON WEBSTER

As this book goes to press the UK government is debating massive reductions in the funding for institutions of Higher Education, particularly in the Arts and Humanities. Coupled with this there are proposals for the raising of fees and new measures for the repayment of student loans. Taken together these proposals have proved so contentious that, for the first time in more than a decade, students and their supporters have taken to the streets in serious numbers. Education is now at the centre of a storm of protest in the UK; it is not clear how it will be calmed, or how trust can be recovered in the politicians and policy-makers who have provoked it.

In the first part of this book we bring together chapters looking in depth at the epistemological grounds for the current loss of trust, arguing that scepticism is more than merely a cynical response to the contemporary decay of trust in public life and that it has its roots in currents of thought deriving from the 17th and 18th Centuries and still influential in contemporary philosophical thought. Those currents are critically considered in the opening chapter, which adopts a straightforward, traditional approach in the account it offers of the development of the history of ideas and values. These ideas and values are then, in chapter 3, re-presented from a post-structuralist perspective. The writing here is demanding. It relies, as Walt Whitman put it in *Democratic Vistas* as long ago as 1871 (Ford, 2011) on

> the assumption that the process of reading is not a half-sleep, but, in highest sense, an exercise, a gymnast's struggle; that the reader is to do something for himself (sic), must be on the alert, must himself or herself construct indeed the poem, argument, history, metaphysical essay – the text furnishing the hints, the clue, the start or framework.

Appropriately for a chapter on the wobbling about that goes with an absence of firm foundations either metaphysical or ethical, the writing in this chapter is allusive rather than expository. As with Derrida and Agamben (see Foster, 2011), whose ideas are everywhere at work in this account, trust is shown as paradoxical, ultimately a matter of choice, resting – if it rests at all – on the have-it-both-ways oxymoron of the law abiding *homo sacer.*

Trust is nevertheless shown to be a deep-rooted social practice, hard to gain and easy to lose, and grounded in shared recognition of civil rights and responsibilities which derive from a social contract. But what if the foundational thinking is itself grounded on assumptions that are unethical? Gillborn discusses the embedding within educational systems of oppressive racist discourse, urging that the systems themselves need to be constantly interrogated so as to uncover the assumptions that will otherwise pass unchallenged, and, to the extent that they encode systematic disadvantage, will breed the student and pupil disaffection and under-achievement as trust is lost. Jameson, approaching the discussion of trust from a different perspective, explores the ways that non-power-holders can exert influence through the way they comment upon the leadership, developing trust in educational leadership in the way it emphasises the responsibilities we all hold in the workplace and the unofficial leadership these responsibilities bring with them: ultimately, we must trust ourselves.

In the second part of the book, the discussion turns to the immediate problems of delivering a reliable and trustworthy education suited to contemporary needs. Europe is one focus here, with Weyringer's call for critical engagement on the part of European youth reinforced by Kaminska's passionate account of the experience of Polish citizens as they move from a Communist social contract to the consumerist world of Western Capitalism. Here, she argues, education has itself taken to the streets, appearing in political street art through which citizens understand and critique their transformation from a communist to a capitalist ideology. Part Two closes with two accounts of the contemporary UK classroom: Gibson and Backus point to the suppression of those student voices whose message the management chooses not to hear – and to the mistrust with which students and pupils respond to this silencing. Children's voices, they argue, need to be heard. Sidorenko closes the book with a more discordant account, arguing against the suppression and silencing, through fear, of voices that would acknowledge the extent of student disaffection.

This book will not by itself restore trust to the world of contemporary education. What we hope is that it will promote a debate that is increasingly urgent, about the loss of trust in education, and the truths and values needed to begin the process of recovering confidence in contemporary education.

References

Ford, M (2011) Petty Grotesques. *London Review of Books*. (March, 2011) p28
Foster, H (2011) I am the decider. *London Review of Books*. (March, 2011) pp31-32

PART ONE: TRUST

1

Truths and Values: education in a cynical and sceptical society

JEROME SATTERTHWAITE

Introduction

This chapter sets out to tell the truth. Two assumptions are immediately evident: that there is a truth to be told, and that it is at least theoretically possible to tell it. Both these claims are contentious, making this chapter highly polemical. They involve taking issue with the powerful strand in contemporary epistemology that abandons the search for truth, encouraging us to celebrate a plurality of 'truths'.

But a word of caution is immediately needed. In what follows I do not try to defend as the way forward the empiricism which underpins the natural sciences, and to brush aside the problems with this sturdy commonsense way of thinking to which post-structuralist approaches have devastatingly drawn attention. I will indeed put in a word for commonsense; but I will avoid the absurd and politically vicious claim that there is an unproblematic route to secure knowledge in the humanities and social sciences and that the procedures of quantitative research are there to show the way. Indeed, though the chapter sets out to tell the truth it will not succeed in doing so.

The claim is not that in the chapter truth will be made to appear, shining clear. Instead, the argument will be that to try to get at the truth is not in itself absurd; and that we are able, by carefully thinking together, to get a sense of the right direction in our inquiries, so as, at the very least, to come to a reasonable agreement about which directions are, simply, wrong. Unless this can be done, we will have no base from which to dismiss with any confidence accounts in the humanities and social sciences which adopt racist, sexist or other distorting points of view, and as regards values no means of telling right from wrong in which we can place our trust. Unless education is to give up on the project of reaching together for a proper view of the social world and some agreed sense of right and wrong, we need this kind of trust.

In this chapter I try to understand and account for loss of trust – trust in people but also trust in ethical and philosophical systems – and to see what can be done to restore it. I want to understand the pervasive cynicism of contemporary Western European cultures about figures in public life, and also the scepticism with which we greet claims for truth and values. In effect, I want to understand why the slogan now appears so often on T-shirts in Poland: *Life is brutal – and full of zasadzkas!* (ambushes). Poland joined the European Union in 2004. As Sieglinder Weyringer points out in a later chapter, one of the chief tasks facing the EU is building a sense of trusting, shared, European citizenship. If the discomforting cynicism of the T-shirt message is what Polish culture has gained as a consequence, the task of achieving a secure epistemological and ethical standpoint is urgent indeed.

There is a practical urgency about the need to restore trust in education. Educators – school teachers, playgroup leaders, lecturers, teaching assistants, headteachers, school managers and educational policy-makers and others – need to be trusted. They need to be trusted to educate, to model and propagate the beliefs and values we as a society ask them to pass on, and they also need to be trusted not to harm or abuse those in their charge and with whom they have an officially recognised relationship of trust. If they are not trusted, confidence in the education system collapses. At the time of writing (December, 2010) a debate in the UK House of Commons is taking place about university tuition fees. Fundamental to the debate is the current public distrust of UK politicians and policy-makers and their promises about education, so vehemently made when election is being sought, so easily discarded later when power was attained: a distrust which is part of a widespread general sense that the political institutions of the United Kingdom are discredited.

Trust in public life

The UK public are cynical. According to Peter Wozniak (Wozniak, 2010)

> By Autumn 2009, trust in British political parties fell to nine per cent, down from 18% the previous year.

Denis Campbell agreed (*The Observer,* 27.9.9):

> Trust in politicians hits an all-time low
>
> Poll sees MPs plummet into last place in public confidence, with business leaders close behind

More generally, Reuters reported (9 December 2010):

> The public's faith in political parties has been sharply eroded during the financial crisis, with four out of five people saying they are corrupt or very corrupt, a survey showed on Thursday.
>
> The 2010 Global Corruption Barometer by Berlin-based watchdog Transparency International (TI) showed that 79 per cent of respondents in a global study believed parties were 'corrupt or extremely corrupt', up from 69 per cent in 2009.

The collapse in public trust is not a solely European phenomenon, and has had catastrophic effects in the United States of America. As recently as 2006, Barak Obama could claim (Obama, 2006:8):

> Not only did my encounters with voters confirm the fundamental decency of the American people, they also reminded me that at the core of the American experience are a set of ideals that continue to stir our collective conscience; a common set of values that bind us together despite our differences; a running thread of hope that makes our improbable experiment in democracy work.

These words sound hollow now; at best extraordinarily naïve. The American public has not reciprocated Obama's trust. A recent website sums up the attitude of increasing numbers of American citizens to their president: *Don't Trust This Man!* (donttrustthisman online). The website flourished during the presidential election campaign – and there was an identical website attacking McCain. Since the election, public trust in Obama seems to have faded. As Krugman put it (*New York Times*, 20th August 2009): *...progressives are now in revolt. Mr. Obama took their trust for granted, and in the process lost it.* Another current web-facilitated phenomenon, the release of thousands of documents, previously classified as secret by the USA, through the Wiki-Leaks site (see *The Economist*, December 2010), will have confirmed the view held by some that diplomats lie *for* their country abroad while politicians lie *to* their country at home.

Trust in public life may be reaching an all-time low; but this is not to suggest that trust has, in the past, been the normal attitude of groups or individuals, whatever their ideological position. For Albert Schweitzer (Schweitzer, 1910), deeply influenced by the German biblical scholarship of his day, and to that extent mistrustful of the mainstream Christian account, Jesus himself was a casualty of misplaced trust: trusting that God would bring the world to an end to save him, he hurled himself upon the cross, and has been hanging there ever since. A less dramatic formulation of the problem of trust, dismal in the extreme in its view of human nature, is given in Hume's (1739) *Treatise of Human Nature*:

> Your corn is ripe to-day; mine will be so tomorrow. It is profitable for us both, that I should labour with you to-day, and that you should aid me to-morrow. I have no kindness for you, and know you have as little for me. I will not, therefore, take any pains upon your account; and should I labour with you upon my own account, in expectation of a return, I know I should be disappointed, and that I should in vain depend upon your gratitude. Here then I leave you to labour alone: you treat me in the same manner. The seasons change; and both of us lose our harvests for want of mutual confidence and security.

This is strikingly similar to the grim view of (uncivilised) human relationships of Hume's arch enemy, Rousseau. Rousseau insists, in a phrase anticipating Orwell, that in the last resort the unco-operative individual must be *forced to be free* (Rousseau, 1955:15); somehow, he thinks, we must be compelled to trust one another. For both these thinkers of the so-called Enlightenment, trust is essential to civil life, and is lacking, and does not come naturally.

Personal trust

Collectively, lack of trust undermines the good order of a society. At a personal level, there is something deeply painful about the breakdown of trust. A marriage has lasted many years; suddenly it emerges that one partner is having an affair. A child has been promised an exciting outing; but on the day, the parents have changed their minds. We have made monthly payments over many years into a life insurance scheme; but the company has failed and our savings are lost. *I thought that love would last forever; I was wrong* (Auden, 1936). There is something childlike about trusting. If we put our trust in someone, we are willing for them to take us in hand and guide us, confident that they will not let us down; and confident, therefore, that they know what they are doing and where they are leading us. When this trust proves to have been misplaced we feel wretched and foolish. Even where there is no person present before us to trust, we imagine an individual (God, Karl Marx, Che Gevara) or a group (the Global Executive Committee of a major bank, the staff of the Accident and Emergency Department of the local hospital) in whose wisdom and care for our well-being we feel we can safely place our trust. We know they may not be able to protect us; but we trust that they are there, trying to help. When this trust is shown to have been unfounded, we feel betrayed; and the more we trusted, so much the more bitter the cynicism which follows the loss of trust. We feel with Ophelia as Hamlet rejects her: *I was the more deceived.*

Trust in Knowledge

The collapse of inter-personal trust is distressing and undermines the ability of the members of a community to work together; but there is a more disabling aspect of the collapse of trust which is fundamentally epistemological – a problem of knowledge. It is the argument of this chapter that there is a long history in Western European culture of decaying confidence in our ability to reach out with our minds to grasp and know the world around us. This decay is paradoxical because it has gone hand in hand with steady advances in the natural sciences. On the one hand, paraphrasing Frost (Frost, 1971:349) our hold on the planet has steadily increased; on the other, we have been urged to mistrust our ability to think beyond the constraints of our culture. Foucault tells us (Foucault, 1970:xv)

> the thing we apprehend in one great leap, that thing that... is demonstrated in the exotic charm of another system of thought, is the limitation of our own, the stark impossibility of thinking *that*.

For Foucault (*ibid*:138) what he calls *designation pure and simple* takes us nowhere beyond the realm of language, incapable of reaching out and grasping the 'order of things'. He insists that

> the description so obtained is nothing more than a sort of proper noun: it leaves each being its proper individuality and expresses neither the table to which it belongs, nor the area surrounding it, nor the site it occupies.

This is inevitable, because (*ibid*:300) language 'curves back' upon itself in the linguistic turn:

> ... there is nothing for [literature] to do but to curve back in a perpetual return upon itself, as if its discourse could have no other content than the expression of its own form; it addresses itself to itself as a writing subjectivity... and thus all its threads converge upon the finest of points – singular, instantaneous, and yet absolutely universal – upon the simple act of writing. At the moment when language, as spoken and scattered words, becomes an object of knowledge, we see it reappearing in a strictly opposite modality: a silent, cautious deposition of the word upon the whiteness of a piece of paper, where it can possess neither sound nor interlocutor, where it has nothing to say but itself, nothing to do but shine in the brightness of its being.

There is a stark contradiction here which demands attention as we struggle with the difficulty of apprehending truth. Foucault is clear that language cannot move beyond itself, cannot, so to speak, pay visits to the world. This is a claim not only about language, but, by inference, about 'the order of things'. Making this claim, there is no hesitation in his tone. He writes as you do when you know, without doubt, that you are right: that what you are telling is the truth. In *The Order of Things* there is no index and no bibliography, giving the impression that his readers do not need, and perhaps should not want, to look beyond the text with which they are confronted. He gives no examples; it is as if examples or illustrations would mislead us, coaxing us beyond the text to a world of ideas beyond it so as to be specific where only generalisation belongs. Reading Foucault – or at least reading *The Order of Things* and *The Archæology of Knowledge*, we are in an impossibly difficult world because we not in the world at all.

What is at stake here is the issue of truth. If language does no more than endlessly recycle itself, we cannot use it to interrogate the world of the natural sciences or the social world of the humanities, and are bereft of the means to spell out even the questions about the social world which trouble us and which we seek to answer. For Foucault, as for Wittgenstein (1958:189), *Whereof one cannot speak, thereof one must be silent.* Richard Rorty, confronting Foucault's linguistic turn, adopts a pragmatist stance, aligning himself with a point of view that offers to solve the problem. He argues that language is a tool and what matters is how we use it. This seems at first glance to offer a way forward from the post-structuralist closed circle. But Rorty is quick to caution us that we should concern ourselves not with what language means but with what are its effects. He tells us (Rorty, 1999:xxiii):

> There is no way in which tools can take one out of touch with reality. No matter whether the tool is a hammer or a gun or a belief or a statement, tool using is part of the interaction of the organism with its environment. To see the employment of words as the use of tools to deal with the environment, rather than as an attempt to represent the intrinsic nature of that environment, is to repudiate the question of whether human minds are in touch with reality – the question asked by the epistemological sceptic. No organism, human or non-human, is ever more or less in touch with reality than any other organism.

To *repudiate the question of whether minds are in touch with reality* is more than a gesture of intellectual despair. It is to abandon the attempt to draw distinctions between competing accounts of the external world, so as to be unable, absolutely and in principle, to tell right from wrong. All accounts of our world – Fascist, racist, sexist, neoliberal, whatever – will then have an equal claim on our acceptance, being no more than examples of *tools for dealing with the environment*, ultimately neither true nor false in any significant way.

Caught between, on the one hand, Foucault's reductive account of language, positioned as it is within the frame of post-structuralist linguistic philosophy and, on the other, Rorty's pragmatic account of language as a tool with no more to offer than any other tool – a hammer, a garlic press – for giving us a means of arriving at a proper understanding of our world, serious thinkers may well feel dismay. Ought we really to *repudiate the question of whether minds are in touch with reality?* It is time to conclude this discussion of trust in knowledge with the appeal to common sense which was referred to in the introduction; and for this we need to turn to Darwin's theory of evolution (Darwin, 1859).

According to Darwin, characteristics that confer on the individuals who possess them an advantage, no matter how trivial, in the struggle for existence, can and do pass on those characteristics to their offspring, who thus inherit the advantage. Over time, the repeated inheritance of the advantageous characteristic preserves a group within a species at the expense of other, less favoured groups. In the struggle for survival, a new species will emerge over time composed of the members of the favoured group.

We can apply this Darwinian account to the problem of knowledge, to make the rather simple, common sense point, that individuals of a species who systematically, or even a few times, had made mistakes about reality, would rapidly have died out. In a herd of antelope, for example, those individuals who correctly recognised a predator and took steps to avoid it would be more likely to leave offspring than the rest, whose less well founded understanding would make them more liable to be taken as prey. Putting this crudely: if for any reason you do not perceive wolves as a threat, and therefore do not take steps to save yourself when wolves appear, you are mistaken. You have got it wrong, and are more likely to be eaten than others in the herd who got it right, recognising the danger, and hence surviving to leave offspring who inherit this useful characteristic.

My claim, at the level of this kind of brutal reality, is that, as regards our ability to know the world around us and to get things right more often than we get things wrong, we must be the offspring of individuals who made less than the average number of serious, life-threatening mistakes. The blunt message of Darwin's theory is that being right rather than wrong about matters of fact is a characteristic that confers a heritable advantage on its possessors in the struggle for survival. This explains why we mostly get things right.

This argument may well seem a preposterous over-simplification. The objection could be made that it takes no account of the complex interconnection that links the thoughts, perceptions and values of each individual to the culture within which, for each one of us, experience and understanding of the world is set. This is a strong objection; but in this chapter we are looking for a basic account that will give support to our need to trust the way we think about and value the world of ordinary social experience. We are seeking a foundational standpoint from which to recover confidence in our thinking. This is a precondition for education: there need to be grounds for holding that an educated account of the social world is to be preferred. Without such grounds, the rationale for education is lost.

I have argued in this section that it is reasonable to trust that human minds are more or less securely in touch with reality. This is, of course, a common sense view; and, for ordinary social purposes, to be trusted. We may rejoin the overwhelming body of the human group on this issue, trusting the sturdy English empiricism illustrated by Dr Johnson kicking a stone into the harbour at Harwich with the famous words 'Thus I refute Berkeley!' (Boswell, 1791:173).

Goethe and Byron – the self as disengaged subject

I have tried in the preceding section to find a basis for the recovery of trust in the way we think about the natural and the social worlds, so as to clear the ground for the more detailed discussion of trust in education which follows in the later chapters of this book. I have suggested that confidence in our ability to reach for truths about the natural and the social worlds may be secured by a return to what I have called the tradition of sturdy English empiricism. This is the tradition of grubbing about in the world around us, sniffing and poking, and kicking stones. In the humanities and social sciences it has been rightly disparaged as insensitive, promoting the reliance on quantitative methods of inquiry that disregard whatever is not easily measured.

Nevertheless, the unapologetic project of the preceding section of this chapter has been to find grounds for the recuperation of trust, at a more fundamental level, in the ways minds work and the understandings they offer. It is time now to turn to the related issue of subjectivity – the focus of attention on the self. Here I will put forward the similarly combative view that we can trace the progress of a narcissistic self-absorption developing over the last two centuries in Western European culture, which, together with the more recent moves in epistemology outlined above, has contributed to the turning away from engagement in the social world of a significant group of theorists and practitioners in the arts and humanities.

Subjectivity has a long and complex history, but emerges with Romanticism in the early years of the 19th Century to become the dominant mode of apperception. Our starting point may properly be Goethe, who in 1806 published the first part of *Faust*. The poem opens with a polemic against words, books and scholarship – all of which are rejected as worthless. What matters is feeling, which should be trusted above all else. In Martha's garden, Faust tells Margareta about love (Goethe, 1987:109)

> Oh, fill your heart right up with all of this,
> And when you're brimming over with the bliss
> Of such a feeling, call it what you like!
> Call it joy, or your heart, or love, or God!
> I have no name for it. The feeling's all there is.

The feeling uppermost in Faust's mind as he says this is sexual. He urges Margareta to give way to the swooning delight of sexual passion and fall into his embrace. This is a familiar trope; what is new is the pre-eminence, at a cosmic level, given to feeling. This was seized upon by Goethe's first readers. They concluded, rightly, that intellectual speculation and the words it uses came last and mattered least in his scheme of things. For Goethe, feelings are pre-eminent; they are God. But a desperate problem remains. Faust wants to get to grips with his world, and do things. He cannot. He cries (*ibid*:48):

> ...though a god lives in my heart,
> Though all my powers waken at his word,
> Though he can move my every inmost part –
> Yet nothing in the outer world is stirred.

He cannot get beyond 'the heart' to engage with the world where things happen. The result is misery:

> Thus by existence tortured and oppressed
> I crave for death, I long for rest.

Faust here is a prototype of the Romantic hero: a male figure who rejects established norms and conventions, has been rejected by society, and has the self as the centre of his own existence. There is a primary focus on his feelings rather than his actions. Although he dreams of heroic action, he is a weary, introspective individualist, rejecting social convention, ill at ease with his world, a wanderer who gets nowhere, an alienated, isolated, melancholy figure, ultimately doomed.

In this he is like Byron's Childe Harold who first appeared in 1812 in *Childe Harold's Pilgrimage* (Byron, 2005). An outcast, disgraced and worn away by his enslavement to passion, he wanders further and further from home, belonging nowhere in society, and longing for huge achievements. He goes beyond convention, reaches out for larger truths, meanings and commitments than the rest of us; and comes to grief: our society is too small for him. His heroic stance makes the everyday world seem dull and humdrum, tame and tepid. He has soared beyond all the triviality and pettiness that detains and directs our ordinary lives.

The appeal of this Byronic hero is, precisely, fantastic: we yearn to be like him, and feel that, deep down, we truly are and that it is only the tedious constraints of the conventional world that get in the way, preventing us from being our real selves, wild and free. This is an early appearance of what will become the hallmark of the Romantic sense of self: a construction belonging in the world of fantasy into which we like to escape. In the real world we fill in the forms, tick the boxes, pay the rent or the mortgage, do the washing up and slow down to thirty when we see the speed camera signs, sustained all along by the sense that essentially we belong elsewhere, in a more exotic and savage milieu. We will go there one day; we are biding our time. In the meanwhile our lives seem mean.

Goethe's Faust and Byron's Childe Harold have moved on from the more sober recognition of Wordsworth, their great predecessor in the early days of Romanticism. In a passage of immense rhetorical power he insists (Wordsworth, 1946:729) that our truths and values and our sense of self need to be based

> Not in Utopia, subterranean fields,
> Or some secreted island, Heaven knows where!
> But in the very world, which is the world
> Of all of us, – the place where in the end
> We find our happiness, or not at all!

This is the commitment that Romanticism was eager to abandon, in favour of fantastic self-absorption. Byron brushed aside the drabness so doggedly affirmed here. His Childe Harold was popularly supposed to be a self portrait of the author. As time went by, Byron did try to connect his fantasy with the world of public events. He came increasingly to model himself on his hero, wearing the clothes, adopting the style, attitude and world view of his creation, attempting to make the real world imitate the fantasies of his imagination. When he died at Missolonghi he was leading a brigade, formed and trained by him, to fight in the cause of Greek independence. He was trying to be Childe Harold, to be his fanciful hero in the real world of public, political affairs. In the mosquito-infested marshland where he was waiting for action, he caught a fever and the doctors bled him to death. Romanticism gave way to bathos: the absurd, small realities bit, diminishing him to a sweating, quivering wreck, who would have done better, perhaps, to have stayed at home, dreamily imagining it all.

Disengagement: 'poets' and 'mechanists'

Fundamental to Romanticism is the sense of a horrible mismatch between what we feel we are and what our day-to-day environment makes us, a dissonance that promotes a process of alienation so as to separate artists, writers, poets, intellectuals and aesthetes into a group of outcasts. The consequence is a shocking disengagement from the real world. In 1842, Tennyson was writing (Tennyson, 1946:299) the kind of sentiments later to be contemptuously rejected by Wilfred Owen (Owen, 1974:37) as *poets' tearful fooling*:

> Tears, idle tears, I know not what they mean,
> Tears from the depth of some divine despair
> Rise in the heart, and gather to the eyes,
> In looking on the happy Autumn-fields,
> And thinking of the days that are no more.

In the same year Edwin Chadwick was presenting to parliament his *Report of the Sanitary Condition of the Labouring Population* (Clayre, 1982:133). He told them:

> After as careful an examination of the evidence collected as I have been able to make, I beg leave to recapitulate the chief conclusions which that evidence appears to me to establish.
>
> First, as to the extent and operation of the evils which are the subject of the inquiry:
>
> That the various forms of epidemic, endemic, and other disease caused, or aggravated, or propagated chiefly amongst the labouring classes by atmospheric impurities produced by decomposing animal and vegetable substances, by damp and filth, and close and overcrowded dwellings prevail amongst the population in every part of the kingdom...

> That the annual loss of life from filth and bad ventilation is greater than the loss from death or wounds in any wars in which the country has been engaged in modern times...
>
> That defective town cleansing fosters habits of the most abject degradation and tends to the demoralisation of large numbers of human beings, who subsist by means of what they find amidst the noxious filth accumulated in neglected streets and bye-places.

There was nothing here about himself or his feelings and the fantasies that sustained them. Two years later Engels described Manchester (*ibid*:122ff):

> Right and left a multitude of covered passages lead from the main street into numerous courts, and he who turns in thither gets into a filthy and disgusting grime, the equal of which is not to be found... In one covered passage there stands... a privy without a door, so dirty that the inhabitants can pass into and out of the court only by passing through foul pools of stagnant urine and excrement...

In 1821 Shelley had remarked (*ibid*:215) that

> Poetry turns all things to loveliness... It transmutes all that it touches, and every form moving within the radiance of its presence is changed in wondrous sympathy to an incarnation of the spirit which it breathes: its secret alchemy turns to potable gold the poisonous waters which flow from death through life; it strips the veil of familiarity from the world, and lays bare the naked and sleeping beauty, which is the spirit of its forms.

Shelley, of course, was talking about minds, not matters of fact:

> All things exist as they are perceived; at least in relation to the percipient. 'The mind is its own place, and of itself can make a heaven of hell...' But poetry defeats the curse which binds us to be subjected to the accident of surrounding impressions...

'The accident of surrounding impressions' was what struck Chadwick, Engels, Oastler and other unpoetic observers, appalled at what they saw before them in the industrialised society of the day. Shelley (*ibid*: 211) sneered at them as *reasoners and mechanists*, precisely because they had lowered their gaze to notice the degradation, filth and squalor in which millions of working people were forced to live their brief lives. The divide is now thoroughly established between the 'mechanists' and the 'poets'.

Baudelaire – the self as disgusting and fascinating

This separation has become nastier by 1857 when Baudelaire, the poet, finds in the spectacle of filth and rottenness not the motivation to leave his study and try to help sort it out, but a range of metaphors and similes for the tormented state of his own and other aesthetes' minds (Baudelaire, 1964:19):

> Packed tight and swarming like a million maggots,
> A crowd of Demons carouse in our brains,
> And, when we breathe, Death into our lungs
> Descends, an invisible river, with heavy wailings.

This is not Engels' Manchester; this is Baudelaire's psyche from which we are to recoil in horror. A rift has opened between the world, operated upon by practical people, concerned with public health, and the mind, dwelt upon in the imagination of the poet, appalled but fascinated by himself. Preparing the way for later analysts of the self – Freud, Proust *et al* – Baudelaire (*ibid*:21) publishes the shocking disclosure that his mother does not love him:

> When, by a decree of sovereign powers,
> The Poet comes into this bored world,
> His mother, terrified and full of blasphemy,
> Clenches her fists toward God, who has pity on her:
>
> 'Ah, why didn't I litter a nest of vipers
> Rather than give birth to this mockery...'

Baudelaire (*ibid*:37) fantasises about being loved by an enormous young giantess. He wants to

> Feel at my leisure her magnificent shape;
> Climb on the slope of her huge knees,
> And at times in summer, when the unhealthy suns
>
> Wearying, make her stretch out across country,
> Sleep without worry in the shade of her breast,
> Like a peaceful hamlet at the foot of a mountain.

It is not hard to understand the impatient rejection of this delicious narcissism by Shelley's 'mechanists' and their successors down to the present day. What shocked Baudelaire's first readers and led to obscenity trials and so forth, was not his disengagement but his fascination with whatever is rotten and disgusting, which he could deploy to represent his private enthusiasms associated with sex and bodies. Here is Baudelaire (*ibid*:45) talking to his lover:

> Remember the object we saw, dear one,
> On that fine summer morning so mild:
> At the turn of the path a loathsome carrion
> On a bed sown with pebbles,
>
> Its legs in the air, like a lubricious woman,
> Burning and sweating venom,
> Opened in a nonchalant cynical way
> her body full of stench.
>
> ....
>
> The flies swarmed over the putrid belly,
> From which emerged black battalions
> Of maggots, which flowed like thick liquid
> Along those human rags.

Prowling around in his mind, sniffing and poking with sickly relish at the images of decay, putrefaction, filth, and so on, Baudelaire has *made use of* the world beyond his mind, to supply his imagination with an unpleasant feast. His is an internalised mirror-image version of Engels' telling us about excrement in Manchester so as to make something happen there for the benefit of the people. Baudelaire tells himself and his readers about filth in order to enjoy the frisson.

Nietzsche – the self as Übermensch, God, Satan

We are sketching in this account a developing separation between two kinds of sensibility and their associated knowledges and commitments. The argument is that, in a mistrustful and cynical society where trust in public figures, but also in shared values and truths, has been lost, it may be attractive to fall back upon a notion of the self – the feeling, intuiting subject, shifting and changing but always recognisable as me – as the final authority for truths and values: a passionately subjective reformulation of Protagoras's (4th Century BCE) *Man is the measure of all things*. These ideas were to be reworked later in the 19th Century by Nietzsche.

Nietzsche's description of a 'free spirit' (Hollingdale, 1981:44) is reminiscent of Baudelaire:

> He prowls cruelly around with an unslaked lasciviousness; what he captures has to expiate the perilous tension of his pride; what excites him he tears apart. With a wicked laugh he turns round whatever he finds veiled ...

There is the same relish as in Baudelaire for the outrageous wickedness which defies conventional morality; but for Nietzsche, the absolute requirement is to be different from the rest of us. The new philosophers he looks forward to (*ibid*:40)

> will not be dogmatists. It must offend their pride, and also their taste, if their truth is supposed to be a truth for everyone... One has to get rid of the bad taste of wanting to be in agreement with many.

The gulf separating Shelley's poets and mechanists has become for Nietzsche the separation between himself and everyone else, especially his readers (*ibid*:19) above whom he towers with measureless superiority:

> As regards my *Zarathustra*, for example, I count no-one as being familiar with it who has not at some time been profoundly wounded and at some time profoundly enraptured by every word in it: for only then may he enjoy the privilege of reverentially participating in the halcyon element out of which that work was born, in its sunlit brightness, remoteness, breadth and certainty... One must be superior to mankind in force, in *loftiness* of soul – in contempt...
>
> One must be accustomed to living on mountains – to seeing the wretched ephemeral chatter of politics ... beneath one...
>
> ...he who is related to me through loftiness of will experiences when he reads me real ecstasies of learning: for I come from heights no bird has ever soared to, I know abysses into which no foot has ever yet strayed...

Nietzsche is the inevitable product of the Romantic fascination with the self which we saw in its earlier stages in Goethe, Byron and Baudelaire. With Nietzsche it reaches what seems at first the end of the road, in the apotheosis of the self. He writes in the manner of adolescent self-absorption. His writing is all in 'MySpace': we are invited to watch him doodling, primping and admiring himself this way and that before the mirror of his writing. There is no logic or development – no coherent argument. What holds his ideas together is the willed conviction that he is himself unutterably fascinating. He has dismissed as beneath contempt anyone who does not see him this way. Such people do not matter, they are worthless. This is in keeping with his notion of himself as the superman, the Übermensch – a new kind of human, as different from ordinary men as they are from the apes. Zarathustra has brought this about (*ibid*:238):

> Behold, I teach you the superman.
>
> The superman is the meaning of the earth. Let your will say: the superman *shall be* the meaning of the earth...
>
> What is the greatest thing you can experience? It is the hour of the great contempt. The hour in which even your happiness grows loathsome to you, and your reason and your virtue also...

From the 1870s onwards, to many serious men and women committed to social change in the interests of fairness, this writing has seemed virtually meaningless. It lacks sobriety, moderation, restraint, the classical concerns that control our interactions with one another, and which pay the interlocutor the compliment of engaging with her or him as adult to adult. Again and again, in reading Nietzsche, we want him to grow up and to engage as an adult with real world concerns. His postures seem childish and embarrassing. But Nietzsche is not going to grow up; he is exultantly going the other way, towards the craziness which ultimately convinces him that he is God, Christ, Satan, everything in heaven and earth. He becomes, himself, the ultimate sweeping statement. To place his trust anywhere else than in his own uniquely astonishing selfhood would be for him a blasphemous mistake.

Proust – The Self in search of itself

It might have been expected that Nietzsche was an impossible act to follow and that after him the road might lead back to the social world of civic engagement. That this direction was not always followed is illustrated some thirty years later by Proust. *A la recherche du temps perdu* (Proust, 1983) was written in a room lined with cork in his apartment in Paris, between 1907 and 1922. The room was lined with cork to keep out the noise of the city. Proust very seldom left that room. People distracted him, and the flowers and trees brought on his asthma. The complete work is 3,300 pages long, well over a million words. It begins, famously, with the central character, who is never directly named, hoping his mother will come to kiss him goodnight (*ibid*:I,13):

> My sole consolation when I went upstairs for the night was that Mama would come in and kiss me after I was in bed. But this good night lasted for so short a time, she went down again so soon, that the moment in which I heard her climb the stairs, and then caught the sound of her garden dress of blue muslin, from which hung little tassels of plaited straw, rustling along the double-doored corridor, was for me a moment of the utmost pain; for it heralded the moment which was bound to follow it, when she would have left me and gone down again. So much so that I reached the point of hoping that this good night which I loved so much would come as late as possible, so as to prolong the time of respite during which Mama would not yet have appeared.

A million words later, the narrator has hardly changed. He has wandered through the world of the fashionable salon, and – of course – down the seedy back allies of the sex vendors, searching, unsurprisingly, for himself. Nietzsche's colossal hubris is absent here, and the social world has made its reappearance; but the self is still the engrossing subject. But where Nietzsche was able to find himself as titanic, radiant with nightmare splendour, for Proust the self, the only serious object of his quest, is lost, *perdu*. His writing is a strenuously detailed record of the long road he has travelled in his search.

It is sobering to recognise that, by the beginning of the 20th Century, a hugely influential and significant group within our culture, composed of artists, poets, novelists and other practitioners of the creative arts and the humanities, exemplified in the examples discussed above, had withdrawn so completely into themselves, had concentrated so exclusively on a private world of anguished feeling, that there was nothing more that could be said by them or about them than that they were lost to the world in the contemplation of their own distress. Romantic subjectivity had led them there, diminishing the scope and range of their concern to that of private nightmare, so that for each of them truth had become 'my truth', almost too distressing to tell – an intensely private and subjective narrative about the writer himself. This could lead nowhere but to anomie, characterised by loneliness and expressing itself in tormented aporia. There was worse to follow.

Hesse and Sartre – the self as outcast

In 1927 Herman Hesse wrote *Steppenwolf* (Hesse, 1965). The protagonist may be a man, may be a wolf; he hardly knows or cares. He is alone and wolfish, a predatory, terrifying other. This is the self not as hero or god, as in Byron or Nietzsche, but as destructive beast. He prowls the streets, wrapped up in himself, enduring a life drained of meaning and significance, prepared only to tell us about it later from behind the closed door of his dingy attic, from which he is about to disappear, no-one knows where. What he sees in those back alleys no-one knows. He never tells us. He is not interested, and he does not expect us to be, in the outside world. What is of interest is himself, the lone wolf:

> I knew that all the hundred thousand pieces of life's game were in my pocket. A glimpse of its meaning had stirred my reason and I was determined to begin the game afresh. I would sample its tortures once more and shudder again at its senselessness. I would traverse not once more, but often, the hell of my inner being. (*ibid*: 252f)

Eleven years later, in 1938, Sartre published *Nausea.* Wikipedia gives this account:

> The Kafka-influenced novel concerns a dejected historian in a town similar to Le Havre who becomes convinced that inanimate objects and situations encroach on his ability to define himself, on his intellectual and spiritual freedom, evoking in the protagonist a sense of nausea.

Once again we are confronted by the private misery of the alienated individual, at odds with himself and utterly out of touch with his social or even material environment, doomed to roam the dark streets alone, for whom *Hell is other people.* This is Walter Benjamin's flâneur, but with all the lights out, all his enthusiasm and all his curiosity drained away, no longer interested in the social world or in the figure he makes in society, loathing the thought of any human contact, in the grip of unbearable meaninglessness: the self as anomie.

In selecting the writers discussed above I have drawn attention to a movement emphasising the self as the proper focus for imaginative attention and I have suggested that the origins of this development may be traced not only to the Romantic movement but also to the philosophical scepticism of the Enlightenment which preceded it, and to which it was, at least in part, a reaction. The result has been a flowering of research and scholarship which privileges discussion of the challenges, paradoxes and problems of doing it, and writing about it, over the ostensible subject matter. The 'linguistic turn' and the ubiquitous concern with the text, or the researcher's 'reflexivity' are, in the terms of this discussion, merely recent manifestations of the trend outlined previously. Anne Carson brings this discussion disconsolately up to date (Carson, 2010):

> you are alone. Whatever idea arises from its knees
>
> ...
>
> will ask of you most of your cunning and a deep blue release like a sigh while using only two pronouns, 'I' and 'not-I'.

The 'I' is where we feel most at home, most sure of ourselves, most able to trust; the 'not-I' is too easily dismissed as incomprehensible, hopelessly distorted through the cultural relativism of our perceptive schema, beyond our power to make real.

Re-engagement

It is time to turn away from the preoccupation of the poetic individualist, engrossed in self-absorption – Carson's 'Isolate' – to see what can and should be done here and now in what Wordsworth calls *the world/Of all of us* by way of social and political engagement. The way forward is spelt by a real-world isolate, Tony Judt, who described his predicament in January, 2010, shortly before his death, like this (Judt, 2010b):

> I suffer from a motor neuron disorder, in my case a variant of amyotrophic lateral sclerosis (ALS)...What is distinctive about ALS... is firstly that there is no loss of sensation (a mixed blessing) and secondly that there is no pain. In contrast to almost every other serious or deadly disease, one is thus left free to contemplate at leisure and in minimal discomfort the catastrophic progress of one's own deterioration.
>
> In effect, ALS constitutes progressive imprisonment without parole. First you lose the use of a digit or two; then a limb; then and almost inevitably, all four. The muscles of the torso decline into near torpor, a practical problem from the digestive point of view but also life-threatening, in that breathing becomes at first difficult and eventually impossible without external assistance in the form of a tube-and-pump apparatus. In the more extreme variants of the disease, associated with dysfunction of the upper motor neurons (the rest of the body is driven by the so-called lower motor neurons), swallow-

> ing, speaking, and even controlling the jaw and head become impossible. I do not (yet) suffer from this aspect of the disease, or else I could not dictate this text.

The isolation here is not fanciful; it is no metaphor. It is also not of his own choosing nor any part of his ideological stance. From his involuntary 'imprisonment' Judt dictated the paper which was published shortly afterwards in expanded form as *Ill Fares the Land*. This achievement serves to illustrate his determined resistance to the process which threatened to cut him off from the social world with which he was, and had for so long been, passionately engaged. It was a determination that was mutual: as he dictated, a complex network of social relationships was operating to enable him to communicate; and an equally complex network of medical support was keeping him alive and well enough to do so. Here was a public intellectual whose engagement with and commentary upon the issues of the day was, more or less literally, his *raison d'être*.

Judt urges us as a duty to maintain this engagement (Judt, 2010a: 237):

> As citizens of a free society, we have a duty to look critically at our world. But if we think we know what is wrong, we must act upon that knowledge. Philosophers, it was famously observed, have hitherto only interpreted the world in various ways; the point is to change it.

For Judt the self-absorption of the Romantic individualist is an abdication of social responsibility. Feelings of metaphysical dread, of alienation and loss, are for him an affliction to be met with whatever resources of stoic resistance we have the energy and will to muster. Such feelings do nothing for us or for the social world with which, as intellectuals, we have a duty to remain engaged. They are no more to be relished, and deserve no higher status, than the creeping dysfunctions associated with ALS. In this he is close to Edward Said who, in August 2004, on the threshold of his own death, thinking about Adorno's analysis of the late works of Beethoven, makes this powerful comment (Said in Rizvi, 2008):

> Like Beethoven, Adorno becomes a figure of lateness itself, an untimely and scandalous, even catastrophic commentator on the present.

and about the later work of Ibsen he writes (*ibid*:4):

> Ibsen's last plays suggest an angry and disturbed artist who uses drama as an occasion to stir up more anxiety, tamper irrevocably with the possibility of closure, leave the audience more perplexed and unsettled than before. It is this second type of lateness that I find deeply interesting: it is a sort of deliberately unproductive productiveness, a going against.

Summarising his account of Said's stance as public intellectual, Fazal Rizvi has this to say (Rizvi, 2008) about Said's 'going against':

> But such re-thinking and revitalisation is impossible unless we learn to speak truth to power. Education has always served multiple purposes, some designed to reproduce existing patterns of power, while others are intended to question them. Education can serve the markets and self-interests of people, as it has increasingly been re-designed to do. But it can equally produce intellectuals who see critique as a form of democratic freedom and who learn the continuous practice of questioning and of accumulating knowledge that is open to, rather than in denial of, the 'historical realities of the post-Cold War world, its early colonial formation, and the frighteningly global reach of the last remaining superpower of today' (Said, 2004:45). It should indeed be possible for a new humanist education to show how, in the past, cultural traditions have interacted with each other and can, more importantly, continue to interact in peaceful ways' (p49). In other words, the role of education should be to provide models of coexistence grounded on a rigorous intellectual approach.

Conclusion – the role of education

In this chapter we have looked briefly at the collapse of trust in the institutions and figures that constitute our social world, at the epistemological struggle to find a trustworthy way of grappling with real-world truths, and at the preoccupation with the self which, I have argued, derives from the decay of confidence in the mind's ability to reach for and apprehend external reality – a decay which has worked, together with the Romantic privileging of the subjective individual as the site of the only true and certain knowledge, to bring about what I have characterised as a species of ecstatic anomie. We have looked at the claims of contemporary public intellectuals such as Said and Judt that there should be no withdrawal from lifelong engagement with the public sphere. We need, in conclusion, to confront the challenge inherent in the argument from cultural relativism, that the public intellectual is able as critic only to rehearse the insights from within the culture which it is her or his project to critique. We need to counter this argument so as to validate the standpoint of figures such as Said and Judt, and to give a rationale for education in the humanities and social sciences.

Of course, the connection between intellectual and academic movements and general public perceptions is seldom straightforward, and to discuss theories and perspectives on the social world is distinct from engaging with that word directly. However, such connections can be made. It is the case, overwhelmingly evidenced in the conference presentations of the Discourse, Power, Resistance conference series and in the publications (including this volume) to which those conferences have given rise, that academics – learners, teachers and researchers – sense that as education becomes increasingly reconfigured along the lines of competitive business, we do not belong here any more; and that to be successful in education we are being required to adopt attitudes and values not our own and which, deep down, we reject. We do not feel at one with the institutions and systems which define our world. We may not be Byronic heroes, or Steppenwolves, or gods like Nietzsche; but we can relate to their disaffection, their sense of not belonging.

At the same time, unless we have resolutely refused to face it, we are confronted by the recognition that as we struggle with what seem to us the problems of making sense of an increasingly uncongenial working environment, there are billions – thousands of millions – of men, women and children, living in conditions of abject wretchedness in the sprawling filth of megacity margins, which have grown up, unregulated, without roads, light, water, sanitation, healthcare provision, education, all over the so-called 'developing' world (see Davis, 2006). We read about disease, destitution, degradation, more or less worldwide, on a scale too huge to imagine; and are forced to acknowledge that this condition – comparable to the state described by Chadwick and Engels in the mid-19th Century – is growing exponentially, year on year. We do not feel at ease belonging to a global system which has this as its consequence. This is not where we want to be, or where we can feel, at home.

We are able to take up a critical stance towards our culture and to confront the increasingly abject misery of the global community, because we are not wholly defined by membership of that culture, that community. We are educated. Education has not detached us from our culture, enabling us to float free of its assumptions; still less should it have coaxed us to disengage. It has, however, given us – and this is always the uniquely distinctive and precious contribution of the humanities and social sciences to the cultures in which those disciplines are embedded – a measure of critical distance. There are other cultures to which our education has given us access; and this has enabled us to adopt a standpoint not wholly subsumed within the mainstream culture of our day. That is the gift of scholarship.

Scholarship is no luxury for a culture. In the UK at the time of writing we are watching the arts and humanities being ruthlessly attacked by government policies that will withdraw funding from them, diverting that funding to the sciences and technology and to the business studies fields where – according to the policy-makers – the returns will be seen in greater competitiveness in global markets. This will have the (intended?) consequence of returning the study of the arts and the humanities to the status of a conversation amongst the members of a privileged elite with the time and money to pursue it – rather like the world from which Castiglione wrote the *Book of the Courtier* in 1528. Education needs to resist this, yet the trend away from social and political engagement in much social science and humanities research has arguably made effective resistance more difficult. By falling into the indulgent embrace of the self and the text and, as a result, becoming less able directly to engage with issues and problems perceived by most fellow citizens, much of the academic and research community has made it easier for both the general public and those in power to ignore what it says. Trust, authority and power are related in complex ways.

The readers of this book have all been trained to think critically and may and should be trusted to do so. This is not as easy as it sounds. Year on year, and brilliantly expressed in April 2010 by David Nutt at the DPR conference in Greenwich, we hear of the more or less unsubtle attempts by those in power to control, redirect or simply suppress the truths they do not choose to hear or that they do not choose to make public. Wikileaks (*The Economist*, 2010) is aptly named: truths often need to be leaked from the powerful interests seeking to contain them. At a time of increasing cynicism, the public intellectual has a point of view, achieved and maintained with sustained hard work, always liable to be overwhelmed, maintained at a critical distance from contemporary culture. The public need to be able to trust that this point of view will be made known. It is the work of education to promote this point of view; this is what education in the humanities and social sciences is all about. If government policy makes this an easy task, that is welcome. But if government policy makes it difficult, so much the more urgently, as Judt insists (Judt, 2010a):

> We need to re-learn how to criticise those who govern us. But in order to do so with credibility we have to liberate ourselves from the circle of conformity into which we, like they, are trapped.
>
> Liberation is an act of will.

References

Auden, WH (1936) Funeral Blues. http://www.love- poems.name/Sad_Love_Poems/Funeral-Blues-sad-love-poemsby-W-H-Auden-Stop-all-the-clocks.html. (accessed 17th October 2010)

Baudelaire, C (1964) *Les Fleurs du Mal*. New York: Dover Publications

Boswell, J (1791) *The Life of Samuel Johnson, LLD* (abridged). London: Penguin

Byron, G (2005) *Lord Byron: Selected Poems*. London: Penguin

Campbell, D (2009) Trust in politicians hits an all-time low. *The Observer*

Carson, A (2010) 'Sonnet Isolate' *The London Review of Books*. 4 November 2010

Castiglione, B (2003) *The Book of the Courtier*. London: Penguin

Clayre, A (ed) (1982) *Nature and Industrialization*. Oxford: OUP

Darwin, C (1859) *The Origin of Species By Means of Natural Selection*. London: Penguin

Davis, M (2006) *Planet of Slums*. London: Verso

Donttrustthisman http://www.donttrustthisman.com/ (accessed 1 December 2010)

Economist, The (2010) The war on WikiLeaks. http://www.economist.com/node/17674107 accessed December 2010

Foucault, M (1970) *The Order of Things: An archæology of the human sciences*. London: Tavistock

Frost, R (1971) *The Poetry of Robert Frost*. London: Jonathan Cape

Goethe, J (1987) *Faust Part One*. Oxford. OUP

Hesse, H (1965) *Steppenwolf*. Harmondsworth: Penguin

Hollingdale, R (1981) *A Nietzsche Reader*. Harmondsworth. Penguin

Hume, D (1739) *A Treatise of Human Nature*. http://ebooks.adelaide.edu.au/h/hume/david/h92t/B3.2.5.html Accessed November 2010

Judt, T (2010a) *Ill Fares the Land: A treatise our present discontents*. London: Penguin

Judt, T (2010b) Night. *The New York Review of Books*, January 14, 2010

Krugman, P (2009) Obama's Trust Problem. *New York Times*, August 20, 2009

Obama, B (2006) *The Audacity of Hope: Thoughts on Reclaiming the American Dream*. Edinburgh: Canongate Books

Owen, W (1974) *The Collected Poems of Wilfred Owen*. London: Chatto and Windus

Proust, M (1983) *Remembrance of Things Past Volumes I-III*. Harmondsworth: Penguin

Reuters (9 December 2010) http://uk.reuters.com/article/idUKLDE6B71VH20101209 (accessed 9 December 2010)

Rizvi, F (2008) Speaking Truth to Power: Edward Said and the Work of the Intellectual. In Satterthwaite, J, Watts, M and Piper, H *Talking Truth, Confronting Power.* Stoke-on-Trent: Trentham

Rorty, R (1999) Philosophy and Social Hope. London: Penguin in Blackburn, S (2005) *Truth: A Guide for the Perplexed.* London: Allen Lane.

Rousseau JJ (1955) *The Social Contract and Discourses.* London: Dent

Said, E (2004)

Shakespeare, W (c1600; 1970) *Hamlet.* London: Longman

Schweitzer, A (1910) *The Quest of the Historical Jesus: A critical study of its progress from Reimarus to Wrede.* London: A and C Black

Tennyson, A (1946) *Poems of Tennyson: 1830-1870.* London: OUP

Wikipedia Nausea. http://en.wikipedia.org/wiki/Nausea_(novel) (accessed December 2010)

Wittgenstein, L (1958) *Tractatus Logico-Philosophicus.* London: Routledge and Kegan Paul

Wordsworth, W (1946) *The Poetical Works of Wordsworth.* London: OUP

Wozniak, P (2010) Trust in British politicians falls to sub-Romanian levels http://www.politics.co.uk/news/legal-and-constitutional/trust-in-british-politicians-falls-to-sub-romanian-levels-$21385569.htm (accessed December 2010)

2

Trust the education system ... to be racist

DAVID GILLBORN

> Trust has to be earned, and should come only after the passage of time. *Arthur Ashe*

Introduction

In this chapter I examine the role of racism in the English education system and argue that, based on previous research and experience to date, the system cannot be trusted to deliver an equitable chance of success regardless of students' ethnic or racial background. Indeed, the system *can* be trusted to adopt procedures and assumptions that are typically racist in their consequences. Subsequent parts of the chapter explore the contribution of Critical Race Theory, a radical new perspective on racism in education, and expose the facts behind the current view (common in media and political discourse) that White working class students are the new race victims. I begin, however, by looking at recent statements of trust in the racially equitable nature of the English education system and its teachers.

Trust, Racism and the Real World

On 12 March 2010 the British National Party (BNP), an extreme nationalist organisation, made headline news in relation to two separate developments. First, a court ruled that its membership requirements were unlawful because they were likely to discriminate: having previously operated a whites-only policy, the BNP had amended its rules to require prospective members to submit to a home visit by party activists who would conduct an interview lasting up to 2 hours (BBC News, 2010a). But it was not all bad news for the BNP because, on the same day, the then-Labour government announced that it had accepted the view of its chosen advisor on the issue – Maurice Smith, a former Chief Inspector of Schools – and decided *not* to bar BNP members from the teaching profession.

Smith was at pains to emphasise the good work of the teaching profession and argued that it should be trusted to deliver on race equality:

> Teachers and their colleagues set out to improve society with a national curriculum at their disposal that explicitly promotes equal opportunities and race equality. There are many examples of how they do this well. In this respect, trust in our teachers and other workers in our schools remains high, and rightly so. That trust should be shared by politicians of all political persuasions; at present, a ban is neither necessary nor proportionate. (Smith, 2010:2)

Police and prison officers are already forbidden to join the BNP but Smith maintained that extending the ban to the teaching profession would be 'taking a very large sledgehammer to crack a minuscule nut' (2010:2):

> Although police and prison officers are banned, to ban more than half a million teachers – or six million public servants – from joining a legitimate organisation would take this to a different scale of magnitude. (Smith, 2010:2)

We should remember that this organisation is led by a Holocaust denier, its deputy leader recently addressed a meeting of European Fascists, and it is 'a party in which many leading activists have criminal convictions, a nazi past or both' (Searchlight, 2009 online).

Smith argued that although 'behaviour that promotes racism is incompatible with membership of the teaching profession' (2010:3) there was no evidence that it was a widespread problem:

> over the last seven years, only four members of the teaching profession, and two governors have been publicly identified as being members of racist organisations and only nine incidents of teachers making racist remarks or holding racist materials have been subject to disciplinary sanction by the General Teaching Council for England. (Smith, 2010:2)

Consequently Smith judged that a ban would be 'disproportionate to the level of risk/prevalence' and that existing measures 'are sufficiently well-grounded and comprehensive to meet the risk' (Smith, 2010:3). The wholly inadequate nature of the existing safeguards was revealed just a couple of months later when a BNP member faced a disciplinary hearing of the General Teaching Council (GTC). Adam Walker was accused of using a school computer to post inappropriate messages online during lessons:

> The hearing was told that in one posting, it was alleged Mr Walker claimed the BNP had risen in popularity because it was 'making a stand' by 'protecting the rights of citizens against the savage animals New Labour and Bliar (*sic*) are filling our communities with'. (BBC News, 2010b online)

Walker was judged to be guilty of misconduct, but only for using a school laptop inappropriately during lessons; the panel were *not* convinced of the seriousness of his postings. The BBC reported that 'Angela Stones, chairwoman of the committee, said: 'The committee does not accept that references to 'immigrants' are of themselves suggestive of any particular views on race'' (*ibid*). Reference to migrants as 'savage animals' does not, therefore, contravene the test of racial intolerance applied by one of the key safeguards that Maurice Smith sees as adequate to ensure our continued trust in the teaching profession. This case is not a one-off aberration of an otherwise trustworthy system: it points to a fundamental weakness in traditional concepts of what racism is and how it operates.

Traditionally, in societies like the US and the UK, both the mainstream media and education policy-makers tend to view racism in a stable and narrow way. Hence, racism is:

- seen as an exceptional occurrence,
- willingly and knowingly enacted,
- motivated by race hatred.

In this perspective, racism might be identified through the use of hate speech or perceived in gross acts of race discrimination, often of a physically violent nature. For example, the murder of Stephen Lawrence – a Black young man stabbed to death by a group of White youths shouting racist obscenities – satisfies even this most limited of definitions (see Macpherson, 1999). However, as the GTC's decision on the Adam Walker case (above) demonstrates, even apparently crude racist language is often excused by hair-splitting and linguistic game-playing: hence, Walker defended his reference to migrants as 'savage animals' on the basis that he only meant *some* migrants:

> 'I have never condemned all immigrants or asylum seekers. My comments relate to those I perceive as coming to our country and committing criminal offences or otherwise behaving badly.' (Adam Walker quoted in BBC News, 2010b online)

In contrast to the narrow, traditional view of racism as meaning only the most obvious and crude acts of race hatred, critical approaches adopt a more nuanced and insightful perspective. Such an approach lies at the heart of Critical Race Theory (CRT), an approach that insists on the importance of understanding racism as it actually operates in the world rather than as an abstract concept to be debated among White power-holders.

Critical Race Theory: a new perspective on an old problem

CRT began as a radical alternative to dominant perspectives in US legal scholarship. It grew in opposition to both the conservative mainstream and the ostensibly radical tradition of Critical Legal Studies (CLS) which, despite its rhetoric, actually gave little serious consideration to the role of race/racism (Crenshaw, 2002). Key foundational CRT scholars include Derrick Bell, Richard Delgado and Kimberlé Crenshaw. Gloria Ladson-Billings and William Tate (1995) first introduced CRT into education and since then a growing number of educators have begun working with these ideas.

There is no single canonical statement of CRT but the approach is broadly characterised by a focus on the central importance of White racism and the need for active struggle towards greater equity:

> Although Critical Race scholarship differs in object, argument, accent, and emphasis, it is nevertheless unified by two common interests. The first is to understand how a regime of white supremacy and its subordination of people of color have been created and maintained ... The second is a desire not merely to understand the vexed bond between law and racial power but to change it. (Crenshaw *et al*, 1995:xiii)

The phrase White Supremacy is used here in a way that is very different to its common meaning: the term usually refers to individuals and groups who engage in the crudest, most obvious acts of race hatred. But for critical race theorists the more important, hidden and pervasive form of White Supremacy lies in the operation of forces that saturate the everyday mundane actions and policies that shape the world in the interests of White people:

> ... a political, economic, and cultural system in which whites overwhelmingly control power and material resources, conscious and unconscious ideas of white superiority and entitlement are widespread, and relations of white dominance and non-white subordination are daily reenacted across a broad array of institutions and social settings. (Ansley, 1997:592)

White Supremacy, understood in this way, is as central to CRT as the notion of capitalism is to Marxist theory and patriarchy to feminism (Mills, 2003:182; Stovall, 2005:247). This perspective on the nature and extent of contemporary racism is one of the key defining elements of Critical Race Theory. CRT views racism as more than just the most obvious and crude acts of race hatred: it focuses on the subtle and hidden processes which have the *effect* of discriminating, regardless of their stated intent:

> CRT begins with a number of basic insights. One is that racism is normal, not aberrant, in American society. Because racism is an ingrained feature of our landscape, it looks ordinary and natural to persons in the culture. (Delgado and Stefancic, 2000:xvi)

When White people hear the word racism they tend to imagine acts of conscious and deliberate race-hatred: discrimination is assumed to be an abnormal and relatively unusual facet of the education system. Such a view is exemplified (above) in Maurice Smith's description of racism in the teaching profession as 'a minuscule nut' (2010:2) not worthy of significant legislative concern. In contrast, CRT suggests that racism operates much more widely, through the routine, mundane activities and assumptions that are unquestioned by most practitioners and policy-makers: what Delgado and Stefancic call 'business-as-usual forms of racism' (2000:xvi). For example, racism figures in the selection and training of teachers, where minoritised teachers tend to have less secure jobs and to teach less advanced classes; in the identification of ability, where both formal and informal forms of assessment encode the assumptions and experiences of White people, thereby disadvantaging minoritised students; and through the selection of curricula that celebrate a false notion of society as colour-blind, where anyone can succeed on the basis of their individual merit: see Gillborn (2008); Gillborn and Ladson-Billings (2010); Tate (1997). This is part of what is sometimes called CRT's critique of liberalism:

> CRT portrays dominant legal claims of neutrality, objectivity, color blindness, and meritocracy as camouflages for the self-interest of powerful entities of society (Tate, 1997:235)

CRT is not critical of the *idea* of a meritocracy (a place where people rise according solely to their efforts and talents) but rather it attacks the *ideology* of meritocracy, ie the false belief that such a state actually exists in places like the US and the UK. In these systems, characterised by deep and recurring race inequity, the pretence of a meritocracy disguises the continued benefit that White people draw from racism and allows race inequities to be presented as just and necessary, as a mere reflection of the deficiencies of the people who suffer racism (Delgado and Stafancic, 2001).

In addition to a focus on racism, CRT is also distinguished by certain other themes. For example, there is a *call to context* which challenges researchers to pay attention to the historical location of particular events and, in particular, to recognise the experiential knowledge of people of colour. CRT does not assume that any group of people can simply read off one 'true' view of reality but there is a belief that people who experience racism are uniquely positioned to understand certain elements of its operation and power (Tate, 1997).

Another distinctive CRT theme is its revisionist critique of civil rights laws as fundamentally limited as a means of addressing inequality. Detractors have sought to present CRT as disrespectful of civil rights campaigns and victories but this is a misrepresentation. CRT is not critical of the campaigns, nor of the people who sacrificed so much to advance race equality (Crenshaw *et al*, 1995:xiv). Rather, CRT looks at the limits to law and policy-making, and shows how even apparently radical changes are reclaimed and often turned back over time. A key element here is the concept of interest convergence (Bell, 1980). Put simply, this view argues that advances in race equality come about only when White elites see the changes as in their own interest. Derrick Bell, the leading African American legal scholar, coined the idea of interest convergence and has summarised the notion like this:

> Justice for blacks vs. racism = racism
>
> Racism vs. obvious perceptions of white self-interest = justice for blacks
>
> (2004:59)

Bell argues that a study of the civil rights movement reveals that time and again the 'perceived self-interest by Whites rather than the racial injustices suffered by blacks has been the major motivation in racial-remediation policies' (Bell, 2004:59). For example, the moves to outlaw segregation in the 1960s are usually presented as a sign of growing enlightenment, but they have to be understood within the context of the cold war and the fact that the US was having difficulty recruiting friendly African states when Soviet interests could point to the forms of apartheid that operated in the Southern US. As the distinguished African American writer WEB Du Bois noted of the famous *Brown vs Board of Education* desegregation case: 'No such decision would have been possible without the world pressure of communism' which made it 'simply impossible for the United States to continue to lead a 'Free World' with race segregation kept legal over a third of its territory' (quoted in Bell, 2004:67). The obvious signs of segregation have gone – such as separate toilets and lunch counters – but the reality continues in economic, residential and educational terms.

Similarly, in the UK, the racist murder of Stephen Lawrence is widely hailed as a landmark case that changed race relations forever. An official inquiry into the police's failure to prosecute Stephen's killers revealed gross incompetence, disregard and deep-rooted racism. Much of the inquiry was held in public and the nightly coverage in the news media meant that the catalogue of police errors and racism was broadcast nationally, initially to a sceptical public but eventually giving rise to a growing sense of outrage. When the inquiry report was published, in 1999, the revelations about the police's arrogance, incompetence and racism were such that inaction by policy-makers was inconceivable (Macpherson, 1999).

The then prime minister, Tony Blair, promised changes in the law and said that the report signalled 'a new era in race relations (...) a new more tolerant and more inclusive Britain' (*Hansard*, 1999:column

380-381). Radical changes were made to race relations legislation; more than 45,000 public bodies faced a new legal duty to pro-actively ensure race equality. All state-funded schools had to design a race equality policy, monitor achievements for signs of bias, and publicly plan to eradicate any signs of race inequity. On paper these are some of the most far reaching equality duties anywhere on earth but in practice they have been largely ineffective because most schools have ignored their duties while the national education department has paid lip-service to race equality but continued to press ahead with key reforms, such as expanding the use of hierarchical teaching groups and promoting a national 'gifted and talented' scheme, that have *increased* the institutional barriers to success facing most Black students in school (Gillborn and Youdell, 2000; Gillborn, 2005, 2008; Tomlinson, 2008).

The Stephen Lawrence case in the UK, like the *Brown* decision in the US, exemplifies the way in which apparently radical civil rights breakthroughs have uncertain consequences in practice. Delgado and Stefancic argue that such events can be seen as 'contradiction closing cases' which heal the gulf between the reality of racism in practice and the public rhetoric of equal opportunities and social justice: '...after the celebration dies down, the great victory is quietly cut back by narrow interpretation, administrative obstruction, or delay. In the end, the minority group is left little better than it was before, if not worse' (Delgado and Stefancic, 2001:24).

Critical Race Theory represents a dramatic break with previous approaches to studying racism in education and is being taken up by a growing array of scholars on both sides of the Atlantic (Dixson and Rousseau, 2006; Gillborn, 2008; Hylton, 2008; Preston, 2007; Yosso, 2006). CRT goes a good deal further than previous perspectives by placing White racism at the centre of its analysis and, for this reason, faces criticism from both sides of the political spectrum:

> CRT's usefulness will be limited not by the weakness of its constructs but by the degree that many whites will not accept its assumptions; I anticipate critique from both left and right. (Taylor, 1998: 124)

Contrary to the caricature of CRT contained in some of its detractors' accounts, the approach does not view all Whites as *uniformly* privileged and racist: all Whites do not benefit equally from White Supremacy but all Whites are beneficiaries of the system to some degree, whether they like it or not. White working class youth suffer multiple educational inequalities, for example, but their interests and cultural identities remain valorised in mainstream politics and culture. In the UK, for example, 'White British' students are expelled at a third the rate endured by their Black Caribbean peers (DfE, 2010:table 12); they are not automatically assumed to be the product of lone parents and chaotic households (Rollock, 2007); and are free from the oppressive focus on cohesion and integration which has become a hallmark of public policy that now views any sign of minoritised identity as a potential threat to national culture and, post 9/11 and the 2005 London bombings, as a threat to security (Gillborn, 2008).

Downside-Up: how the White working class became the new race victims

> School low achievers are white and British
> *Times*, 22 June 2007
>
> White boys 'are being left behind' by education system
> *Daily Mail*, 22 June 2007
>
> White boys 'let down by education system'
> *Daily Telegraph*, 22 June 2007
>
> Deprived white boys 'low achievers'
> *Daily Express*, 22 June 2007
>
> White working-class boys are the worst performers in school
> *Independent*, 22 June 2007
>
> Half school 'failures' are white working-class boys, says report
> *Guardian*, 22 June 2007

These headlines relate to a report on low educational achievement (Cassen and Kingdon, 2007) and repeat a focus that resurfaces at regular intervals whenever statistics are published on low achievement. This focus is familiar to anyone who works on race equality: it characterises media debates on the issue and has become a feature of almost every discussion with education professionals on the issue. Before considering the statistics behind these kinds of debate, I want first to examine the public discourse of White educational failure because this recurring storyline (and its attendant assumptions) have important and destructive consequences educationally, politically and socially.

This is how a leading daily newspaper reported the publication of official statistics on GCSE attainment:

> **White boys falling behind**
>
> *White, working-class boys have the worst GCSE results*
>
> ... Just 24 per cent of disadvantaged white boys now leave school with five or more good GCSEs.
>
> This compares with 33.7 per cent for black African boys from similar low-income households.
>
> There were fears last night that the figures could hand votes to the far-Right British National Party because additional funding is available to help children from ethnic minorities. (*Daily Mail*, 13 January 2007)

There are several things to consider here. First, the misleading assertion that 'additional funding is available to help children from ethnic minorities': in fact, local authorities (LAs) and schools have to *bid* for dedicated funding towards minority education projects: the additional funds are not simply handed out, automatically privileging minoritised children as the story seems to suggest. Second, the story argues that the results could fuel support for extreme political parties like the BNP. This repeats a line of argument that has featured in British political discourse since the late 1950s – when riots by White racists led to the first major immigration controls (Ramdin, 1987). By warning of the danger of inflaming support for racist parties, what actually happens is that politicians and commentators invoke the threat of racist violence as a means of disciplining calls for greater race equality. This can be seen clearly in the following quotation from the specialist educational press:

> Cameron Watt, deputy director of the Centre for Social Justice and a key figure involved in a report on the subject published recently by former Tory leader Iain Duncan Smith, said: 'There's a political lobby highlighting the issue of underachievement among black boys, and quite rightly so, but I don't think there's a single project specifically for white working-class boys. I don't want to stir up racial hatred, but that is something that should be addressed.' *Times Educational Supplement*, 12 January 2007

It is important to recognise what is happening here. Official statistics reveal that most groups in poverty achieve relatively poor results *regardless* of ethnic background. As Figure 1 illustrates, the achieve-

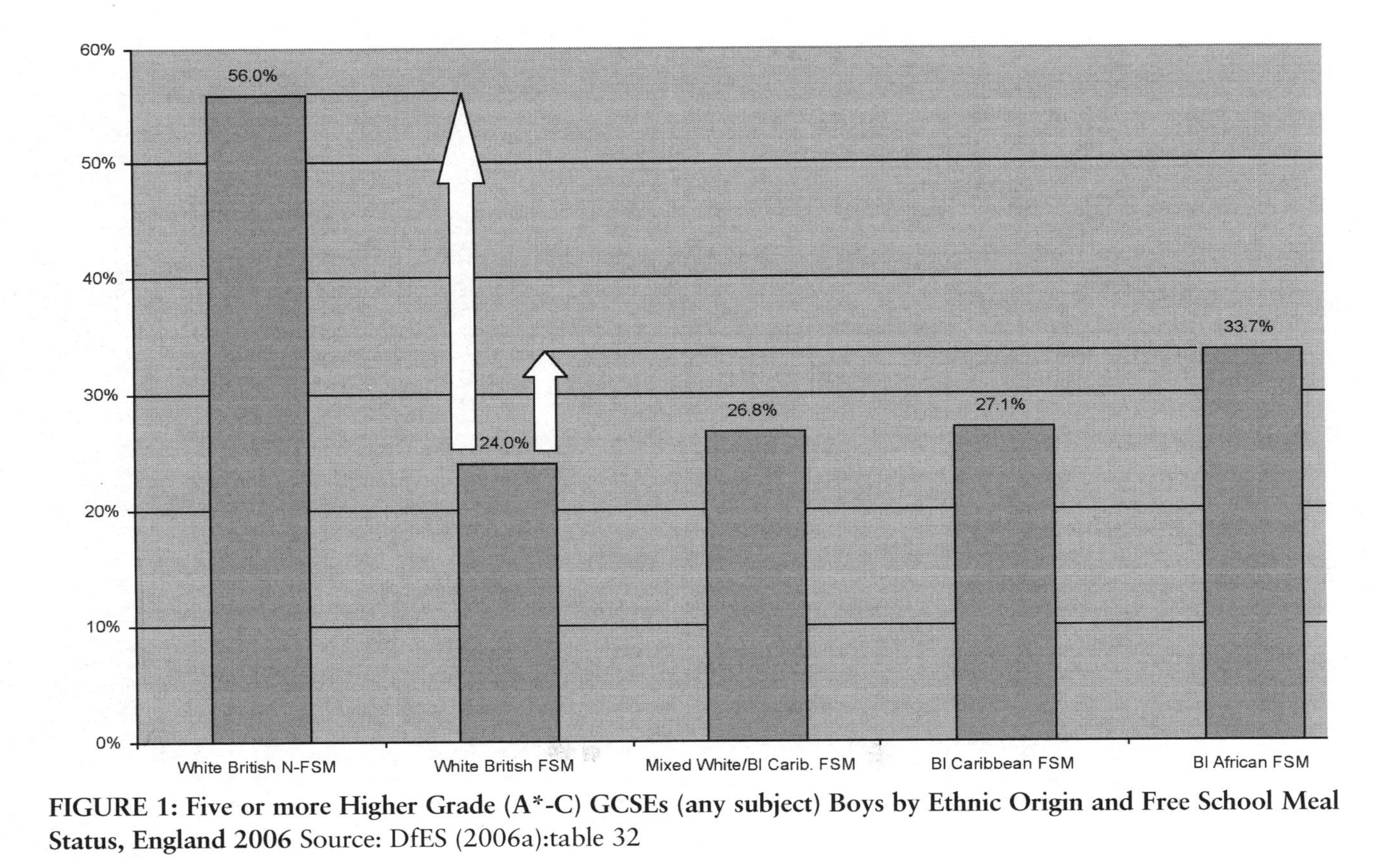

FIGURE 1: Five or more Higher Grade (A*-C) GCSEs (any subject) Boys by Ethnic Origin and Free School Meal Status, England 2006 Source: DfES (2006a):table 32

ment gap between White students in poverty (in receipt of free school meals – FSM) and more affluent Whites (N-FSM) is more than *three times* bigger than the gaps between different ethnic groups who are equally disadvantaged: there is a 32 per cent point gap between N-FSM and FSM White boys, compared with a 9.7 per cent point gap between FSM White boys and the *most* successful of the Black FSM boys (categorised as Black African). And yet it is the race gap that is highlighted both in the *Daily Mail* story (above), which warns of BNP mobilisation, and in the attendant story in the *Times Educational Supplement*. It is significant that despite the larger socioeconomic inequality, media commentators and policy advisers do not warn of an impending class war: they do not raise the spectre that failure on this scale will promote action against private schools or the 'gifted and talented' scheme that receives millions of pounds of extra funding and is dominated by middle class students (see Gillborn, 2008). The race dimension is deliberately accentuated in the coverage.

The media image of failing White boys goes further than merely highlighting a difference in attainment, it actually includes the suggestion that White failure is somehow the *fault* of minoritised students and/or their advocates. This is implicit in the quotation attributed to Cameron Watt (above) but is also an explicit part of some media coverage. This can be seen by examining some of the radio coverage from an award winning news and current affairs programme: the *Breakfast Show* on BBC Radio 5Live.

Radio 5Live is a national channel run by the BBC. It was re-launched as a dedicated news and sports service in 1994 and has been described as 'one of the success stories in the recent history of British broadcasting' (Tolson, 2006:94); in 2010 it was named 'Station of the Year' in the annual Sony Radio Academy Awards. The BBC enjoys exceptionally high levels of public trust in relation to its news content; recently receiving more than *five times* the rating of its nearest rival in a survey of public opinion (YouGov, 2005). This makes the BBC's news coverage potentially very influential because it is the most trusted news provider and caters to a national audience. In addition, the programme in question, the *Breakfast Show*, is held in high regard professionally: it won the Sony Radio Academy Award for the Best News and Current Affairs Programme (Sony, 2007).

On 22 June 2007 the programme led its news bulletins with the story that fuelled the numerous headlines already quoted (above) on White boys as the key under-achieving group. At around 6am Nicky Campbell, one of the programme's two main hosts, interviewed a researcher who was introduced as having contributed to the research report behind the headlines (all quotations from Radio 5Live are my own verbatim transcriptions from an audio recording of the programmes. I use standard transcription notations: (...) denotes that speech has been edited out; *italicised* text denotes that the speaker stressed this word/ phrase):

> Nicky Campbell:
> 'Isn't the problem that – the race relations industry has, some would argue, *compartmentalised* people. And if we had less concentration on race, more on *individuals*, we took colour out of the equation: it wouldn't be 'oh Black boys do this, White boys do that, Chinese boys do this, Asian' – it should just be looking at children as *individuals*. Isn't race part of the problem here in a sense?'
>
> Interviewee (a member of the research team):
> 'Yes you do have to look at children as individuals but, but this kind of research does actually *show* erm that people from different cultures are having different experiences...'

Despite the host's suggestion that 'the race relations industry' is somehow culpable, therefore, the researcher maintains that ethnicity is an important variable and should not be removed from policy debate. Around an hour later the same issue led the 7am news headlines and was explored in an interview with a London headteacher:

> Nicky Campbell:
> '...there's the inescapable conclusion, according to some of our listeners, a- a-and indeed according to some experts too, that the school system has been focusing *disproportionately... too much* on children from other ethnic backgrounds.'
>
> Interviewee (a London headteacher):
> 'I, I think, if I'm being honest that probably was true years ago, it's not the case now, we are – we're put in a position where schools have *got* to focus on all of the data. We're very *data rich* across education and we are accountable for the educational attainment of all of our students.'

The host's analysis was now backed by the invocation of 'some of our listeners' and 'some [un-named] experts too' but again the interviewee failed to support the idea that White kids suffered because of minoritised students in their schools. In fact, the London headteacher seems to argue that the government's emphasis on 'accountability' has raised standards for all. Unfortunately, as research has shown, different groups of students have *not* shared equally in the overall improvements that both Conservative and Labour governments have highlighted in the headline attainment statistics. In particular, White working class and Black students of all class backgrounds have not shared equally in the improvements (see Gillborn, 2008; Gillborn and Youdell, 2000).

Undeterred, at 8am the same topic featured in the news headlines and was explored with new guests, including Professor Gus John (one of Britain's leading campaigners on race equality):

> Nicky Campbell:
> 'Some are saying that too much attention has been given to African and Caribbean boys to the *detriment* of young white boys.'
>
> Gus John:
> 'Well the facts don't bear that out you see. An-and I think this discussion is pretty *distorted*, certainly as far as facts are concerned...'

The interviewee steadfastly rejected the proposal that White boys' low achievement was somehow the fault of Black students. But the damage was already done. Listeners and un-named 'experts' had been cited to support the argument and its constant repetition made it a key aspect of the morning news broadcast. At 9am the *Breakfast Show* was followed by an hour-long phone-in on educational failure and the presenter read out a familiar sounding view:

> Presenter: (reading from listeners' text messages)
> 'Somebody else says, er, 'White youngsters fail because PC [politically correct] teachers and the media are more interested in Black and Asian children.'

In this way the country's most trusted news service had effectively promoted the view that White children are the *victims* of ethnic diversity in general and race equality in particular.

A tendency to present White people as the race victims has been commented upon by writers in both the USA (Apple, 1998; Delgado and

Stefancic, 1997) and the UK (Rollock, 2006). The particular manifestation of White victimology in recent academic, media and political analyses of examination performance is especially dangerous for several reasons. The discourse presents Whites as the victims of race equality measures. Consequently, moves that have been inspired by a commitment to social justice become recast as if they represent a competitive threat to White people; they are redefined as a sectional, racialised, even racist, campaign. Simultaneously, this refrain of racial competition has the effect of erasing from sight the possibility that members of all ethnic groups might excel in a single educational system. The prominence given to these arguments and the strategic citation of far right groups (such as the BNP) has the clear effect of sounding a warning to everyone involved in education: *make sure that White kids are well catered for – don't let race equality go* too *far*. The threatened price of de-centring White children is racial violence – both symbolic (in threats and insults) and physical. It is known, for example, that racist harassment often increases after prominent news stories on race issues. In the run up to the 2001 General election, for example, it was reported that 'Officers in the Race and Violent Crime Task Force, set up after the Stephen Lawrence inquiry, said they were shocked to discover a direct relationship between political rhetoric, such as Tory leader William Hague's 'foreign land' speech, and an increase in attacks on asylum-seekers (Ahmed and Bright, 2001:1).

Race, Class and Educational Attainment

In the previous section I noted how the educational attainment of 16 year-olds was reported in the British media as revealing a situation where, in the words of the *Daily Mail* newspaper '*White, working-class boys have the worst GCSE results*' (13 January 2007). It is clear from the data summarised in Figure 1 that the inequality of attainment between 'White British' boys in receipt of free school meals and their White peers who do not receive this benefit (N-FSM) is considerably larger than the difference between White and Black FSM boys. Nevertheless the *Daily Mail* story accurately, if selectively, reported the statistics:

> Just 24 per cent of disadvantaged white boys now leave school with five or more good GCSEs. This compares with 33.7 per cent for black African boys from similar low-income households. (*Daily Mail*, 2007)

It is significant that the paper chose to highlight the largest possible Black/White inequality: Black African FSM boys were 9.7 percentage points more likely to attain five higher grades, ie three times the size of the gap between White British and Black Caribbean FSM boys, which stood at 3.1 percentage points. Even more importantly, the story focused exclusively on pupils in receipt of free school meals but used a variety of terms as shorthand for this group, including working class, disadvantaged and low-income. This is a common feature of media coverage of educational statistics. Indeed, this assumption that FSM equates to working class students was enshrined in some of the headlines quoted earlier:

> White working-class boys are the worst performers in school
> *Independent*, 22 June 2007
>
> Half school 'failures' are white working-class boys, says report
> *Guardian*, 22 June 2007

This slippage, from receipt of free school meals to working class, may be an innocent attempt to bring life to otherwise verbose and dry educational statistics. But the consequences of this shift are far from innocent. Receipt of free school meals is used as a crude measure of disadvantage in educational statistics mainly because it is a piece of information that is readily accessible: the data are routinely collected by schools and provide a simple binary division. In contrast, there is no single scale of social class categories that is universally recognised; the categories are multiple and difficult to interpret; and, perhaps most importantly, the data are expensive to generate because additional, often sensitive, information is required. Consequently, official research rarely uses a detailed measure of social class, preferring instead to rely on the simple proxy of FSM.

In the GCSE data quoted above, 13.2 per cent of all pupils were in receipt of free school meals (DfES, 2006a:table 32). But in a recent survey by the National Centre for Social Research more than half of UK adults (57%) described themselves as 'working class' (BBC News Online, 2007). Consequently the discursive slippage from free school meals to working class has the effect of inflating the significance of the finding: data on a relatively small group of students, 13 per cent of the cohort, are reported in a way that makes it appear descriptive of 57 per cent, more than half the population.

The focus on pupils in receipt of free school meals has become increasingly pronounced in recent years. The media's exclusive use of the FSM statistics reflects the way that the data are presented by the Education Department itself. In 2006, for example, the department published a 104 page digest of statistics on race and education (DfES, 2006b). Amid the nineteen tables and 48 illustrations, the document focuses a good deal on the significance of the FSM variable and, for example, includes *three* separate illustrations detailing different breakdowns of GCSE attainment among FSM students (DfES, 2006b:65-68): in contrast there is not a single table or illustration giving a separate breakdown for N-FSM students and their relative attainments cannot be deduced from the FSM data that are presented.

The failure to interrogate N-FSM attainment in official documents invites the question as to how different ethnic groups attain within this larger, increasingly neglected, 86.8 per cent of the cohort. The answer is contained in Figure 2 overleaf. As the figure illustrates, the image of White failure created by the newspaper headlines does not reflect the reality as experienced by the majority of students. White British students who do not receive free meals are more likely to attain five higher grade passes than their counterparts of the same gender in several minoritised groups, including those of Bangladeshi, Black African, Pakistani, Mixed (White/Black Caribbean) and Black Caribbean ethnic heritage.

Clearly, race inequality of the more familiar variety (where minoritised students achieve less well) remains a key characteristic of the English education system and affects students of *both* genders. Students of Chinese and Indian ethnic heritage are the only principal minority groups who are *more* likely to achieve five higher grade passes than their White N-FSM peers – see Gillborn (2008: ch.7). The largest inequalities relate to Black Caribbean N-FSM students, where girls are 9.7 percentage points less likely to achieve the benchmark than their White peers and the figure for boys is 17.2 percentage points.

The significance of the 'White under-achievement' mantra was highlighted when the then-Labour Government released a new race equality strategy in January 2010. The document argued that race equality could not be addressed in isolation from other forms of inequality (Department for Communities and Local Government (CLG), 2010: 12) and emphasised the need to take account of White sensitivities –

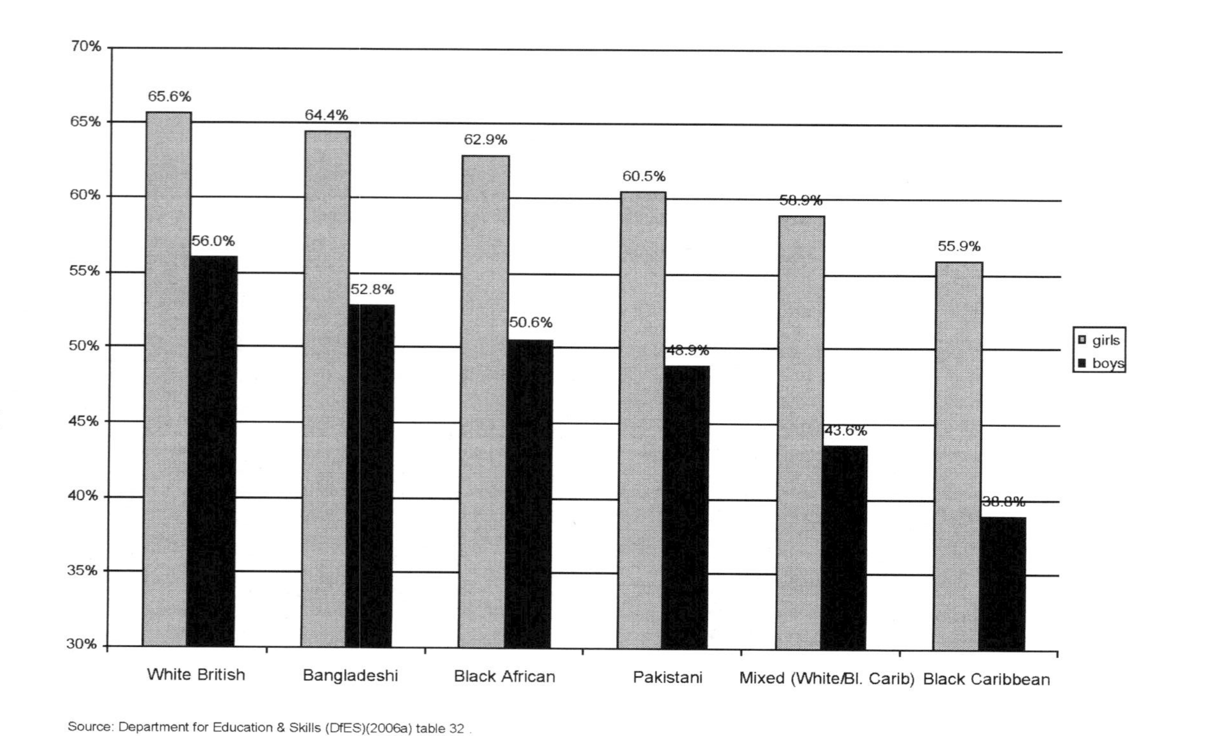

Source: Department for Education & Skills (DfES)(2006a) table 32 .

FIGURE 2: Five or more Higher Grade (A*-C) GCSEs (any subject) Non-Free School Meals by Gender and Ethnic Origin, England 2006

yet again using the BNP as a reason to ensure that White interests remain centre stage:

Racism is also achieving a political voice through the British National Party (BNP) and other extreme racist groups. These groups seek to exploit legitimate worries (...) there is a risk that our efforts will be exploited by those who would distort them to drive people apart [...] No favours. No privileges. No special interest groups. Just fairness. (CLG, 2010:10-12)

A document that was meant to set the tone for future race equality work, therefore, downplayed the importance of racism, highlighted socio-economic factors, and placed the concerns of the White majority centre stage.

Conclusion

The English education system consistently operates in ways that are patterned by systematic raced, classed and gendered inequities. In recent years there has been a pronounced tendency in research, political and media discourse to portray White working class boys as the most disadvantaged group in school. I have shown that this image is based on a mis-reading of educational data which focuses on students living in poverty and receiving free school meals (around 13% of the cohort) and then generalises their attainments as if they applied to all those who consider themselves to be 'working class' (more than half the population). This focus has the effect of blaming minoritised students and their advocates for class inequity and renders further race equality work redundant.

At the same time, a minimalist traditional notion of 'racism' is assumed in policy discourse; this view sees racism as simple, crude and obvious. Hence the complex and widespread racist structuring of inequity via teacher assessment, selection and disciplinary procedures is simply not considered. Rather, a very narrow interpretation is applied, one that fears generating support for the BNP by being over-zealous while finding no evidence of racism, even where a BNP teacher posts foul propaganda during school time, as in the Walker case discussed previously.

This is the state of racism and education in England. The only rational approach, in view of past inequities and current policy assumptions, is to trust the system to continue to operate in systematically racist ways. Our task, as critical educators, is to expose these processes and to work to disrupt them.

References

Ahmed, K and Bright, M (2001) Labour failing to meet pledges on race, *Observer*, 22 April, p1

Ansley, FL (1997) White Supremacy (And What We Should Do about It). In Delgado, R and Stefancic, J (eds) (1997) *Critical White Studies*. Philadelphia: Temple University Press

Apple, MW (1998) Foreword. In Kincheloe, JL, Steinberg, SR, Rodriguez, NM and Chennault, RE (eds) *White Reign: Deploying Whiteness in America*. New York: St. Martin's Press

BBC News Online (2007) What is working class? http://news.bbc.co.uk/1/hi/magazine/6295743.stm (accessed 6th August 2010)

BBC News (2010a) BNP membership rules still discriminatory, court rules. http://news.bbc.co.uk/1/hi/uk_politics/8564742.stm (accessed 6th August 2010)

BBC News (2010b) BNP activist cleared of intolerance on online comments. http://news.bbc.co.uk/1/hi/england/8703184.stm (accessed 6th August 2010)

Bell, D (1980) Brown v Board of Education and the interest convergence dilemma. *Harvard Law Review* 93 p518-533

Bell, D (2004) *Silent Covenants*. New York: Oxford University Press

Cassen, R and Kingdon, G (2007) *Tackling low educational achievement*. York: Joseph Rowntree Foundation

Communities and Local Government (CLG) (2010) *Tackling race inequality: a statement on race*. London: CLG

Crenshaw, KW (2002) The First Decade. *UCLA Law Review*. 49 (5) p1343-1372

Crenshaw, K, Gotanda, N, Peller, G and Thomas, K (eds) (1995) *Critical Race Theory*. New York: New Press.

Delgado, R and Stefancic, J (eds) (1997) *Critical White Studies: Looking behind the mirror.* Philadelphia: Temple University Press

Delgado, R and Stefancic, J (2000) Introduction. *Critical Race Theory: the cutting edge*. Philadelphia: Temple University Press

Delgado, R and Stefancic, J (2001) *Critical Race Theory: An Introduction*. New York: New York University Press

Department for Education (DfE) (2010) *Permanent and Fixed Period Exclusions from Schools and Exclusion Appeals in England, 2008/09*. SFR 22/2010, London: DfE

Department for Education and Skills (DfES) (2006a) *National Curriculum Assessment, GCSE and Equivalent Attainment and Post-16 Attainment by Pupil Characteristics in England 2005/06 (provisional)*. SFR 46/2006, London, DfES

Department for Education and Skills (DfES) (2006b) *Ethnicity and Education: The Evidence on Minority Ethnic Pupils Aged 5-16. Research Topic paper: 2006 edition*. London: DfES

Dixson, AD and Rousseau, CK (eds) (2006) *Critical Race Theory in Education*. London: Routledge

Gillborn, D (2005) Education policy as an act of white supremacy: whiteness, critical race theory and education reform. *Journal of Education Policy*. 20 (4) p485-505

Gillborn, D (2008) *Racism and Education: coincidence or conspiracy?* London: Routledge

Gillborn, D and Ladson-Billings, G (2010) Critical Race Theory. In Peterson, P, Baker, E and McGaw, B (eds) *International Encyclopedia of Education*. Volume 6, Oxford: Elsevier.

Gillborn, D and Youdell, D (2000) *Rationing Education: policy, practice, reform and equity.* Buckinghamshire: Open University Press

Hansard (1999) Prime Minister's Questions, 24 Feb 1999: column 379-387 http://www.publications.parliament.uk/pa/cm199899/cmhansrd/vo990224/debtext/90224-20.htm#90224-20_spmin0 (last accessed 3 May 2007)

Hylton, K (2008) *'Race' and Sport: Critical Race Theory*. London: Routledge

Ladson-Billings, G and Tate, WF (1995) Toward a critical race theory of education. *Teachers College Record*. 97 (1) p47-68

Macpherson, W. (1999) *The Stephen Lawrence Inquiry*. CM 4262-I. London: The Stationery Office.

Mills, CW (2003) *From Class to Race*. New York: Rowman and Littlefield

Preston, J (2007) *Whiteness and Class in Education*. Dordrecht, Netherlands: Springer

Ramdin, R (1987) *The Making of the Black Working Class in Britain*. Aldershot: Wildwood House

Rollock, N (2006) Legitimate players? An ethnographic study of academically successful Black pupils in a London secondary school. Unpublished Ph.D. Thesis: Institute of Education, University of London.

Rollock, N (2007) *Failure by Any Other Name?* London: Runnymede Trust

Searchlight (2009) BNP deputy leader addresses international fascist rally. http://www.searchlightmagazine.com/index.php?link=BNP-deputy-leader-addresses-international-fascist-rally (accessed 6th August 2010)

Smith, M (2010) *Maurice Smith Review: a review of the measures to prevent the promotion of racism by teachers and the wider workforce in schools*. London: Department for Children, Schools and Families

Sony Radio Academy Awards (2007) The News and Current Affairs Programme Award. http://www.radioawards.org/winners/?awid=74andawname=The+News+%26+Current+Affairs+Programme+Awardandyear=2007 (accessed 6 August 2010)

Stovall, D (2005) Forging community in race and class: Critical race theory and the quest for social justice in education. *Race Ethnicity and Education*. 9 (3) p243-259

Tate, WF (1997) Critical race theory and education: History, theory, and implications. In Apple, MW (ed) *Review of Research in Education*, Vol. 22. Washington DC: AERA

Taylor, E (1998) A Primer on Critical Race Theory. *Journal of Blacks in Higher Education*. 19 p122-124

Tolson, A (2006) *Media Talk: spoken discourse on TV and Radio*. Edinburgh: Edinburgh University Press

Tomlinson, S (2008) *Race and Education*. Maidenhead: Open University Press

Yosso, TJ (2006) *Critical Race Counterstories Along the Chicana/Chicano educational pipeline*. New York: Routledge

YouGov (2005) *Press Gazette Poll: The most trusted news brands*. London: YouGov

3

Wavering Conditions of Trust and Resistance

RUTH L. SMITH

The social contract comprises a familiar discourse of claims on trust and resistance, formulating how to think-identify-enact society. The language travels widely. Even when not directly contractual, many agreements of modern societies evoke gestures of trust, mistrust, and resistance by which contract-like concerns for rights, obligations, and consent are in play. While often rejected, the discourse of contract often finds elaboration in rejection as well as in confirmation when Anglo-European speakers and writers specify moral-social-geographic regions and routes by agreement and disagreements with its terms. As that most conserving genre, contractual grammar operates by designating an idea of clear propositional terms whose exercise signifies citizen membership but which membership also requires.

That social contracts can depend on the syntax they claim reliable is predicated, by convention, on their ability to manage the violence that lies in and of a discourse of governing. All the more reason that contracts provoke suspicion: for ordering firmness and for allowance conditions, permeable to new confidence and new resistance, not neutral but shape-shifting, yet held by something that writers and speakers move with and move toward.

Those who contrast the self-defined solidity of modernity with the liquidity of the present would argue that terms of contract and society reside with the artifacts of the modern past (Bauman, 2000; Přibáň, 2007). While contract propositions would seem to be the most stable of artifacts, they include the anxious and the wayward in consent, autonomy, and argument; not all is solid. At the same time, reference to modern agreement traditions marks late modern and current talk, albeit making other ways. That contractual reference continues to circulate prompts my interest in tracing what I call wavering conditions, not only more than speakers and writers can say but more that they do say, for better and worse, ill-defined and well-defined in variance, irresolution, or the differently resolute. By taking as given modern motions as lure and concern and by sensing contractual discourse as motion, negotiations of trust, mistrust and resistance show up not only in propositional lines but in wavering, as if in unsettled cultural overtones.

Wavering may seem difficult to recognise though it's generally right at hand rather than out of sight. My purpose isn't to make a case for a contract philosophy of wavering but to notice measures of motion in theoretical, political, and everyday contexts that remain close to contract in writing by saying more – bending, adding, warning or reminding in remarks on power, danger and opportunity. Intervening in modern discourse, Derrida observes that Rousseau marks all writing as dangerous in its representation as sign, but notice that it's the genre of contract writing, whether education or contract proper that suggests the danger to Rousseau that Derrida picks up on (1974:144). The history of liberal and Marxist critiques articulates the dangers that contract relations only ratify market relations with which people negotiate or attempt to negotiate their societal lives and persons, the contract as a reflexive discourse of commodity abstraction and reduction seeking other markets.

All wavering isn't the same but any following along its momentum would have to stop short with the consolidated realist view that all power entails the known compromises of society or with the diffuse view that eschews the political in the unknown irresolution of all language. Taken strictly, both responses presume that there is nothing else to know, just more of the same. In contrast, wavering points to even slight turns in grammar that can make a crucial difference. Someone moves something by argument, identity, and travel across places, indicating propositional mobility that may include: contingency in logic; relying on saying yes and no at the same time but at different registers; assigning idea-affective outlooks to political identity; marking noncitizen identities; allowing movement, constraining movement, and forcefully moving people around. Let me say more about contracts and then move to specific instances of negotiating by wavering conditions.

When confronted with propositions that want strengths of logic and politics, postmodern readers are quick to pick up on uncertainties of trust that mediate differences and proximities of contracting discourses. Social contract writers propose fluctuations of political discourse, not just to assure trust and displace mistrust but to commandeer mistrust and resistance with rules about making a way around that may be familiar, may change a society overnight, or may challenge it over long struggles for a just social reconfiguration. Nonetheless, we resist and contracts also hesitate: hesitation that is at once incorporated but not entirely domesticated, producing a further decision about contracting options that may be subtle or outright in advancing human actions amidst constraints. To consider that these options aren't all the same reduction puts the idea of wavering at an angle from Agamben's (1998) view that willy-nilly contracts impose the single law of imperially governed violence, while keeping an eye on the bare life that Agamben traces, with reference to Hobbes's contract.

Famously and infamously, Hobbes initiates an early modern contract firm about a discourse of power that proposes trust by way of the social – linguistic arrangements of the body politic. According to Hobbes's civil texts (1650, 1651), society emerges in the discourse of contracting relations with consent by subscription, but having written out a means of signifying power that requires consent to sovereign authority, Hobbes gives away as well that contracts are argued rather than self-evidently rational, contingently marked rather than absolute, and uncertain in linguistic exchange. Weber's (1946, 1958) modern notion of citizen and society wavers in an idea of ambiguity tied to membership alienation and resignation; for Weber the wavering of citizenship constitutes the autonomous conscience capable of political and moral decision.

Each of these early modern and modern bids for a discourse of society carries forward commitments to rule and role of authority that we reject for good reasons. While rejection stays in play, curiously, the discourse doesn't go away in two further moments when writers of contracts address and reconfigure wavering in civil trust and resistance: Derrida (2001) who engages Kant with rights of immigration and Martin Luther King (1986) who engages civil promises with rights of travel. These contractual claims manage discursive features of trust and mistrust, building in resistance that, in turn, prompts more writing.

If we make wavering a contractually relevant term, no more and no less, we can notice moral and political burdens in struggles of cultures; that wavering keeps taking us to those burdens makes us want to have done with contracts, never to inquire into them again. Rather than converse with antipathy simply to separate between good and bad contracts or between acceptance and rejection of contract idea, schema of wavering indicate a milieu of imbricated ordering and disordering, as people state what a reality seems to be, test the waters and take chances, including mortal chances. Notions of never indicate unsettled routes of vacillations with designations, blurring with specificity, ambiguities with rules.

While humans construct language modes, they exert demands that affect language production. Requirements of contract writing and of writers can coalesce, slide by, or step back from each other, neither genre nor inventor just as they please. The contract exerts rhetorical demands and the writer wants to claim something, which, again, may be the wish that the demands go away only to neglect the force of a decided contract in its wavering conditions that others have unexpectedly reached for or we unexpectedly need. Wavering narrows and expands trust and mistrust in the immediacy of day to day life. Is it safe to cross the street?

The term contract pertains to a number of institutions and is itself an institution, a culturally variant structuring that can enforce as law, remind us of connecting and disconnecting powers, and philosophically tell us a great deal though never enough about how we recognise others, and are, in turn, recognised by them. It is as if social contracts are the father called enlightenment society trying to tell us who we are. We know they can tell us something, but what is it? Currently, ideas of agreement emerge with declarations of human rights that pressure only slightly the most horrendous of contracts for torture or slavery. Conflicts between region and individual take place as nations flounder with rights that elude the control of nation-state, as they always did. The first property rights were the contracts best secured for individuality and every other move toward contract right as member or citizen has required the resistance of trespassing on someone's ownership.

An open but not unsupervised question lies in the wavering idea of agreement as willing, wanting, hoping, counting on, going on as if to agree, doubting. Agree, we say, with reservation, all things being equal, which of course they are not. Long records of agreements show that human beings have arranged overlapping contracts in matters of trade, kinship, religion and social governance. But the modern practice in its English language claims, with its host of religious and civil legacies, emerges with the social contract that from the seventeenth century forward identifies the powers of modernity as a phenomenon called society, increasingly as nation-state. If the contract once spoke for some as the modern account of the legitimating signatory of trust, its sovereignty is now difficult to pin down. We start within the middle of things, having already broken an original contract with the beginning, of which there are many.

By way of Augustine, Arendt (1996) says that out of original disobedience we make ourselves historical with no going back. Let's go on to say that every day we start in the middle of things, with working questions about contract hesitations: what is covered by this insurance benefit, with whom can I argue about this charge, what office can authorise this request, how must I identify myself? For Arendt the historical world is where 'all live together as a matter of course' (1996: 103). But how to speak-write-think politics under next or new conditions that no one trusts enough to sign on to? To a great extent, contract talk continues because of this quandary.

Part of the quandary is that by inheritance the contract artifice of consent courts mistrust, with confidence and unease; the artifice of contract wavers in worry over the initiating move to consent and so tries to provide universal benefit if all agree at once, or else some will have to risk agreement while others hang back, a worry about promises among individuals and among nations. Contract discourse knows it jeopardises itself in needing powers and persuasions of agreement, attention, will and desire to follow through with what it wants more of: consent to itself as the mode of consent. Not even Hobbes's absolute sovereignty can guarantee the contract and resolve its hesitations about itself, but the absence of guarantee doesn't disguise contractual power to distribute differentially and insistently.

In *Rough Crossings* (2006) historian Simon Schama chronicles promises of land ownership for free and slave African people who had fought with the British against American colonists, had waited for passage in Nova Scotia, and who finally travelled to Sierra Leone. Their causes pressed by their British leader John Clarkson clash with other abolitionists and members of the Sierra Leone Company who, in England, conduct a mobile semiotic of making, evading and breaking promises in agreement less to freedom and more to an anti-slave trade, but widened commerce with its accompanying Christian conduct (Schama, 2006). John Clarkson isn't reappointed to leadership but Nova Scotian Africans and John's brother Thomas Clarkson persist against mistrust from those Africans who doubt the British and against mistrust from the British who doubt the Africans; for a time the new community holds out amidst its own and British competing claims (*ibid*).

In addition to new agreements about the freedom of slaves, wavering conditions anticipate failures to agree and asymmetrical positions of agreement hierarchy. In 2005, a young woman able to make her way home gives an account of her sexual slavery in central Europe, saying of the transaction, in translation: 'we guessed that we were being sold but we hoped that we were wrong' (Bienstock video, 2005).

No social contract discourse is more associated with mistrust and less associated with resistance than that of the early modern Hobbes, whose war of all against all examines the consequences of no agreement to civil discourse and announces the anxiety of all contracting. Early modern wavering takes place as the aftermath of civil wars and as a venture into new discourses in a plurality of competing views from people engaged with identifying political authority with linguistic reference. Though for Hobbes violence is discursive as argument and narrative, reading *Leviathan* could leave one to wonder why a contract is possible at all.

Hobbes is the materialist philosopher of matter in motion but also suggests links with Wittgenstein, who wants to relieve things of assigned stasis and muteness by inquiry into anything that indicates making a way, the grammar we produce with certainty, uncertainty, query, and sometimes by hitting bedrock. Immediately, scepticism enters in without owning the metaphysical control of uncertainty in how we get around; Hobbesean mistrust points to political scepticism as a working sensibility rather than an essentialised position of meaning. While he adheres to a large-scale ordering determinism, may we read him less squeamishly. But does the scepticism extend to sovereignty, or does

Hobbes mistrust sovereign power enough? These are questions in his discourse of society, which, more than any other contract, presents society as discourse. A persistent wavering condition of contract lies in the need to confirm itself by reaching outside itself to secure terms of unwavering – the Restoration King, parliament, the Enlightened Monarch, the moral law, moral sentiment, the military.

Hobbes also wavers. Minimally, he advises the sovereign power to be reasonable rather than exercise brute authority in making judgments. In this and other propositional ventures Hobbes says more rather than less in designating civil discourse with moves that attempt to domesticate mistrust without entirely resisting it. He indicates that to do politics is to argue well with logic, vigour, and a mind for the counter-argument and without holding to rejections of argument in religious dogmatism or scientific self-evidence. With a proposition that isn't absolute and argument that is contingent as human construction, the author most identified with absolute rule says that speaking-writing society requires relinquishing absolute starting points and conclusions.

Further wavering conditions emerge when Hobbes (1650) indicates that we have difficulty understanding each other, and that one historical time has trouble understanding another. If linguistic capacity doesn't secure transparency of understanding, the capacity for speech nonetheless earns Hobbes's (1651) admiration, making possible signs by which to give definition and recall to thoughts so that we can reason by determining words and their relations in argument. In spelling out positions of slave, servant, parent, gender and ownership, *Leviathan* distinguishes qualifications for subscription membership amidst a fraught array of power relations that the contract incorporates and exposes.

Hobbes writes with early modern concern for publicity of truth and a philosophical view that meaning isn't private nor is it privileged among the male classes. We want to sort out Hobbes so that we trust him or we don't. Instead the contract insists on motion within and among its lines in which arguments don't settle themselves, nor can force settle them though force can be decisive; people make arguments and they're never done. Along with the momentum of invention and concession in a discourse of contention and obedience, Hobbes indicates wavering conditions of restlessness when propositions, his and ours, show that we recognise several things at once not easily separated, reconciled or set aside. One reason we're not done with Hobbes lies in the shared search for civil discourse when we know we can't escape our own arguments nor do we think we can anticipate with much acuity argument's on-going political motions.

Writing a later modernity, Weber (1946) wavers differently. An agreed-to mistrust and resistance characterises the figure of the rational, unmarked, alienated citizen whose capacities and attitudes include the wavering of inner resignation, compromise and ambiguity. Weber formulates these dynamics in a self-reflexive vocabulary and syntax by which modern society articulates itself to itself. To cultivate inner discipline and disposition, one's willingness to engage in the political can't be distracted by irrational and nonrational affective relations among humans. And one must abide the institutionalised technical processes that now cut off human engagement from a wider natural world, an existential situation of disenchantment understood most particularly among those persons of high modernity defined in this contract-like discourse of society and power.

While Weber's sociological method attempts to establish objectivity and interpretative understanding, in the German context his analysis assigns priority to state authority as the legitimate agent of force in a bureaucratic society (1946). In civil life, the ascetic heroic figure negotiates these fields as a discourse Weber finds inevitable rather than arguable; while looking for the moral moment of conscience, he is more or less sure what can be said, and he has already evaluated it (1946).

In other words, Weber's critical assessment of modernity as rationalised, individualised and abstracted from relationships indicates political agreement as to what modern society has asked of members and criteria as to what constitutes political membership action, but in stating these aspects as if they were requirements he presents an absolute discourse of modern society. In the wavering of bringing higher purposes to the lesser values of politics, including society itself, an already decided hesitation provides official identities to citizen and state, identities that can and indeed must claim their ambiguities.

Weber registers another move with an idea of brotherhood composed of those whose association allows for the genesis and cultivation of western cities. Shifting institutionalising agreements develop on the bases of ownership and belief among commercial and political figures, willing to break from older ties to secure protection for new economic and political arrangements and negotiate conflicting interests, such as those in Europe among the capitalist merchant classes that distinguish themselves from the feudal nobility while drawing on the fraternal relations by which brotherhood retains and releases monastic reference (1921).

The modern city bears the imprint of earlier notions of responsibility that Weber now combines with individual autonomy to carry a burden of obligation but without relations; Weber retains an authority line from father to son and yet advances the modern rejection of the paternal. Found only among men who are citizens, the social imaginary of brotherhood leaves no mark of membership identity, a condition that wavers as contradictory and clarifying. Weber's typifications of urban autonomy formation and secular asceticism overlap in other wavering conditions that establish civil membership.

Despite his support for women's emancipation and participation in civil office, especially from German Protestant middle classes, Weber analyses women as a group bound by unreliable emotional ties of familial and religious loyalties that limit autonomy. While assuming individual Jews to be within German civil society, Weber designates Jews as a group bound by traditions of family and observance, outside the unmarked space of assimilated modern societal discourse.

A hierarchy of hesitation indicates a hierarchy of mistrust. Hesitations over the untrustworthiness of modern society authorise hesitations about those untrustworthy under criteria of autonomy and even more so under criteria of assimilation to nation-state governing a ranking of citizen individual, society, women and Jews. Weber's account of individual and group interests, impersonal order, and membership in well-defined conditions draws society as a modern grid where ambiguity too exerts control, the proper ambiguity assigned the autonomous civil actor and the improper ambiguity assigned those defined by groups. Rigid as it is, however, the grid wavers with uncertainty in its disenchantment with society and with nature.

Questions of contract discourse prompt questions of obligation that are entangled with aspects of obedience and promise. If one pursues the course of citizen life – say, political argument and concern for the social body from Hobbes and political stance by compromise and conscience from Weber – one accepts a process that is by their characterisations wavering, given agreements to a society taken as warned. Even if the sovereignty of monarch, parliament, conscience or state is negotiated, society is still restless and in search of security itself. Hobbes and Weber both write their discourses of society by asking us to agree to more than any argument can sustain. In fact, all political discourses ask for more and promise more even when they are modest; even when we are critically sceptical. To be able to cross the street is an expression of civil life in motions we want to take for granted, not even to raise to the level of considered condition, much less agreement or promise. Did I agree to surveillance? Do these cameras promise security?

Social contracts identify matters in motions authorising who can move from one side of the proposition to the other and who can configure civil moving. The modern idea of motion that moves across freely involves the physicality of rights-bearing claims and the discursive character of individual and group access and participation. The immediately sensate and the highly abstract discuss and distribute each other as conditions of hesitation that wouldn't necessarily be hesitant in consequence.

Just as there are places that invite leisurely wandering by modern impulse, I want to say that there are places no one wants to go because they are so wrong in their inhumanity and unreliability (as international accords agree), but I must say that someone goes there, not only but including us in the United States. When there, contracts collapse in the deep order and disorder of their violence; their sentences deliver a trust no one can give, because it bespeaks unaccountable political power, and a mistrust no one can get rid of because it bespeaks giving up governing the situation at all.

These possibilities and impossibilities of governing order and disorder contribute to the terror imposed on those undergoing the torture of threatened and inflicted torture and torturous imprisonment on the part of states that found and unfound themselves by democratic contract. Surely agreements to terror and torture in all quarters visited on any quarters would bring an end to chances of trust in any societal discourse, to such an extent has consent lost its moorings. Further conditions apply, for part of the violence that worries all contracting relies on wavering that can by suggestion and secret hint expand and contract far more than anyone wants to say publicly. Under wavering conditions of privacy someone may move toward lenience or severity and if we know what is happening, then it's no longer private, though much information is privately held as an agreement to mitigate intervention. Given the discursive incredulity of the social contract for its violence or suppression of revolt, mistrust pushes into resistance to taking anything at its word; contracting would seem to bring language to a stop or to demonstrate how language comes to a stop. In the resistance, contracting discourse goes on with wavering conditions, among them travel and hospitality because there is more to address; and the contract persists with that more.

In a section of Kant's social contract *On Perpetual Peace*, first published in 1795, he writes that 'Cosmopolitan right shall be limited to conditions of universal hospitality' (1983:118). With this idea Kant argues that everyone should be able to travel as a guest under terms of hospitality and the cosmopolitan, a claim he also puts in the negative to say that one should not be treated as an enemy when arriving in another's country so long as he behaves peacefully; in turn, even if rejected, he must be treated without harm. Derrida enters the discussion with a matter of immigration agreements, by which particular cities identify themselves as places of residence opened to immigrating populations (2001:4).

Kant specifies the hospitality to the foreigner or alien as a contractual rather than philanthropic matter, with the designation of right and the further designation of justice. By comparison Derrida speaks of the injustice when 'civilized nations in our part of the world' behave brutally toward those considered not to count, thinking about shippers who in their 'inhospitable' commercial interests abuse and cruelly enslave native peoples on the Spice and Sugar Islands as if the lands were not their habitation (2001:119). Derrida writes of hospitality as a juncture of the language of Kanttaken Enlightenment and the late modern cosmopolitan language of contract agreements.

Derrida folds claims for immigration and residence into Kant's moral law, that we act universally rather than with exception. Indeed, says Derrida, what could be more sovereign than the exception? In pressing forward with the immediate, Derrida asks his readers to consider the civil possibility without wavering – that immigrants be received with the right to be accorded hospitality as guests who can live there as inhabitants rather than as those who must move on. But at this point Kant withholds the firm hand of the moral law given the compromised, self-interested state that agrees most of all to the momentum of its own conditions. Derrida withholds the anxiety of the absolute responsibility he has taken up and set down to move forward without Kant's conditions that cosmopolitan rights address only visiting, not residence (residence for Kant is an agreement of charity) and that such rights fall under state control (2001:20-22). Questioning not Kant but himself, the anxiety wavers another way, Derrida wondering if he can fulfil the residence question with a discourse of cities, committed without the sovereignty of an absolute or its ambiguity.

Perhaps it is unlike Derrida to agree that politics loses its moorings under the sway of deconstruction, but he has acknowledged as much when he takes up Rousseau to notice that the contract needs other parts of speech to keep its agreements, namely the supplement. The supplement adds to contract invention to show that Rousseau must adopt a kind of anomalous reasoning in order to move from one idea of civil society to another. Civil society is the natural bond among humans, or it is what is ruined by division and rule, yet civil society can't be thought of in natural terms, but is instead born of its ruined terms, for there is no unruined society before society as there was no language before grammatical divisions and rules. Contracts actively supplement themselves as themselves. The supplement holds the place as substitute and is empty and filled with the sign for something itself (1974:144).

Speech is natural and writing is not; nature and society each enrich and endanger the other. As written, each mistrusts the other but can't reject the other; the writing is ambidextrous: with two hands, one agreed, the other disagreed, unable to write without just agreeing or disagreeing. It is exhausting and inexhaustible that one move is necessary to move the other. In hesitation, Hobbes writes with two hands at least, while Weber writes with one hand in ambiguity. Kant can't write his way to practical public law without the unwritten ideal of right in agreement with what, he writes, only nature makes possible. All contracts waver but their conditions of wavering aren't the same.

Untrustworthy, the contract is unavoidable for Martin Luther King's wary trust, King who prefers the covenant of divine-communal obligation and love but who also engages national conflict to take apart slave-contract rule from the social contract rule that too late might remember its promises. King draws from a number of discourses to argue against civil agreements to waver and dismiss, hesitate and reject the claims of African-Americans to move across. In the drama of the speech *I have a Dream* it may be remembered that King speaks of the defaulted promissory note regarding 'life, liberty and the pursuit of happiness' (1986:217), but it may be forgotten that in later paragraphs he supports the call to continue walking ahead with a bill of particulars that starts with a problem of travel. '...our bodies heavy with fatigue of travel, cannot gain lodging in the motels of the highways and the hotels of the cities. We cannot be satisfied as long as the Negro's basic mobility is from a smaller ghetto to a larger one' (218). In order to travel to the Lincoln Memorial, many at that August 1963 event would have gauged intricacies of local law that made crossing city and state lines dangerous in their slender variance about the wrong place to stop to eat or sleep.

The difficulty of travel also weighs among King's concerns in the earlier written document of April 1963, *Letter from Birmingham City Jail,* when, in a lengthy proposition expressing the violence and insult of racialised society, King includes having to sleep in your car because no motel will allow you a room (293); access counts among the agreements of modernity that mobility requires a resting point so that mobility may continue. As King says in the 'Letter', unjust law requires the just address of nonviolent protest in which moral claim supercedes the legal in order to bring segregation to an end and confront lines of racial boundaries that inscribe cultural, as well as legal, consent.

In bringing forward agreements to prohibit movement, King in effect lets those who didn't already know that he, like all African-Americans, asks himself: will I be arrested if I inquire about a room or will I be shot if parked off the road to sleep in my car? King proposes a principled high road that finds all contracts lacking in their lesser political promises, even when fulfilled, while he indicates that law has a higher political road that social contracts make available. He doesn't hesitate over the difference between present and ideal reality, but wades into the wavering possibilities of what law can contribute to freedom, to the removal of segregation's racialised contract for a society that says yes but no.

Segregation in the United States and Apartheid in South Africa count among those legal-cultural names that identify moving peoples with mixtures of law, mistrust and danger: slave trade, separation, reservation, refugee, ghetto, immigrant, migrant, alien and permit. Indices of nation and the foreign identify each other by allowances for entry; in the Anglo-European past, for instance, French Huguenot to England, Jews to Denmark or indentured servants to the American colonies. Gestures of confining motion for those marked 'foreign' accompany assumptions that natives stay home, although the distinction is made more complex when considering guild practices that kept craftsmen walking across borders and trade routes that kept seafaring men away from home (Walsted, 2003). At the same time, the mobilities of societal place are restricted and unpredictable as people seek to contend with or improve their lot by moving, finding more hierarchy than right, more struggle to survive than an improved future that contract promise would seem to assure. In *Guests and Aliens*, Saskia Sassen (1999) documents immigration that over the eighteenth and nineteenth centuries characterises European culture to an extent often not acknowledged. Speaking of new migrating populations of workers in the industrial nineteenth century, Sassen observes that social mobility is limited:

> In this the condition of the new migrants approached, again, that of the political refugees. ... The geography of movement became a vector of change without a secure destination. They revolved on fortune's wheel rather than pursued a fate (Sassen, 1999:45).

The conditions cast in terms of permanent motion include that no one in motion warrants trust without a place of residence. The contract is a place of membership residence that trusts with mobility those who count as citizens, and mistrusts those who are mobile when they have been assigned no place except the one for which they were bought or to which they were brought. In measures distinct from refugee or immigrant, contracts of slavery precede and follow wavering conditions in allowances of who can go where.

Sometimes terms conflate: African American residents of New Orleans now consider themselves refugees forced to flee from the disasters of flood and civil neglect. Sometimes terms separate: Frederick Douglass in England fleeing charges of complicity in Harper's Ferry is freed by law when British supporters pay his then owner Hugh Auld who sets the manumission price at 150 pound sterling or 711.66 dollars (Douglass archive).

The juridical invites mistrust; yet without it, Derrida argues, the unconditional remains pious and remotely sovereign, itself a dangerous authority (2001:23). Contracts do more than ask us to consider in general by asking us to consider, really, what about this afternoon? In King's *Letter* he asks, when writing in jail about Socrates and Tillich, about why strategic resistance can't wait for metaphysical time, about his daughter forbidden access to the amusement park. If left to vagaries of political compromise or antinomies of things that can't be changed, the social contract lacks the immediacy and authority that King wants and which he trusts can come of the *Declaration of Independence*, although he knows it has not. *The Declaration* wavers.

Wavering conditions aren't outside or marginal but are part of what goes on in any agreement; so we have to look further into what we've agreed to, for the language states more or less than we thought. Contract terms link the most immediate matters of trust with the uncertain claims of high concept yet current conditions of wavering undermine all discourse to ask again: when will the torture end, will I be sold, may I live in this city without hiding? Derrida wonders about the sovereignty of the city – sovereignty of which he is suspicious, although it possibly provides a place of agreement apart from the rule of nations. Mobility and residence hesitate before each other in unsettled networks of old and new culture and law.

Like opera, the contract is not a pure form, a reason for its attraction or at least its possibility in unease and invention. To speak of contracts is to acknowledge one artifice and look for other experiments in how persons talk and move democratically – not a list of issues, but what we enact as grammar seeking more grammar. Wavering conditions aren't outside or marginal but are part of agreement that goes on under many circumstances. What it is to reside and to move, where to find work and the work one finds, are all paths of contractual entanglement and evasion in postmodern law and culture.

Where we are going and by what terms is a part of any agreement that the agreement never entirely measures, yet contracts consign walkways and we want as much as always to cross the street in safety. A contract assures itself to protect its own wavering; it cautions, and someone goes across anyway. The consequences could be terrible or they could be fine but are now without the trust that we want to assume whenever we can.

Practiced and unpracticed, the contract implicates us in the deep power structuring of the young woman's statement about herself and other women from her area who were promised work some distance from home: 'We guessed we were being sold but we hoped that we were wrong' (Bienstock Video, 2005).

If argument and ambiguity mark earlier politics and earlier wavering, signs of travel have become emblematic of re-contracting the political; in one way or another all coming and going is the subject matter of twenty-first century contract and all contract marks coming and going. We might consent or we might resist in hopes of something else to-morrow. Social contract writing as we know it comes from confidence and vulnerability, hope and fear, the inscription of violence and prohibition of violence. As a discourse among others, each instance prompts particular hesitations. While perhaps we could once move them to the side to be taken for granted or to be rejected, contractual discourses continue to circulate differently in many registers, some seeking freedom from contract and some seeking safety with an accord; all merit attention to the motions of their wavering conditions.

References

Agamben, G (1998) *Homo Sacer: sovereign power and bare life*. Stanford: Stanford University Press

Arendt, H (1996) *Love and Saint Augustine*. Chicago: University of Chicago

Bienstock, R (2005) *Sex Slaves*. Boston: PBS WGBH/Frontline Documentary

Bauman, Z (2000) *Liquid Modernity*. Malden MA: Blackwell

Derrida, J (2001) *On Cosmopolitanism and Forgiveness*. New York: Routledge

Derrida, J (1974) *Of Grammatology*. Baltimore: Johns Hopkins

Hobbes, T (1650) Human Nature and De Corpore Politico. In Gaskin, JCA (ed) (1994) *Human Nature and De Corpore Politico*. Oxford: Oxford University Press.

Hobbes, T (1651) *Leviathan*. In Schuhmann, K and Rogers, GAJ (eds) (2003) Leviathan. London: Thoemmes Continuum.

Kant, I (1983) *Perpetual Peace and Other Essays on Politics, History, and Morals*. Indianapolis: Hackett

King, ML Jr (1986) I Have a Dream. In: Washington, J (ed) *The Essential Writings and Speeches of Martin Luther King, Jr.* San Francisco: Harper

King, ML Jr (1986). Letter from a Birmingham Jail. In: Washington, J (ed) *The Essential Writings and Speeches of Martin Luther King, Jr.* San Francisco: Harper

Přibáň, J (ed) (2007) Liquid Society and Its Law. Aldershot: Ashgate

Sassen, S (1999) *Guests and Aliens*. New York: The New Press

Schama, S (2006) *Rough Crossings: Britain, the slaves and the American Revolution.* New York: HarperCollins

Walsted, AL (2003) Guest Workers in Denmark – Migration, Work and Identity. In: Walsted, LM and Ludvigsen, P (eds) *Migration Work and Identity: A history of European people in museums.* Copenhagen: Worklab-Arbejdermuseet

Weber, M (1958) *The City.* Glencoe, Ill: The Free Press. (Weber, Posthumous, 1921).

Weber, M (1946) Politics as a Vocation. In: *From Max Weber: Essays in sociology.* New York: Oxford University Press. (Weber, 1919).

4

Dance like a butterfly, sting like a bee: Moments of trust, power and heutagogic leadership in post-compulsory education

JILL JAMESON

Introduction

The boxing similes 'dance like a butterfly, sting like a bee', derived from the popular misquotation of Mohammed Ali's celebrated description of his boxing technique – *Float like a butterfly, sting like a bee* – applied to educational situations, refer to informal, authentic breakthrough moments of trustworthy leadership that occur every day in organisations at all hierarchical levels, taking people forward to achieve beneficial outcomes, despite barriers and tensions. Such moments of dazzling virtuoso leadership, sometimes humorous, sometimes poignant, always authentic, 'dance' to inspire others. They can also 'sting', speaking truth to power with harshly accurate critique at times when others are too frightened to speak. They occur spontaneously and the leaders enacting them may be anyone, though some individuals tend be the authors of such moments more than others.

Traditional interpretations of leadership sometimes reductively envisage that leadership resides only at the top of educational organisations, inevitably the sole property of elite managers with positional authority. In this view, leadership is seen as a powerful capacity to act and influence, a possession controlled and dispensed by authoritarian leaders, who bestow – or not – favours or sanctions of their office upon followers. In a commodified transactional education system, the dance of leadership may be a dutiful, performative march: followers are coerced to fall in line in promoting educational goals closely tied to marketable material achievements.

The culture of educational leadership in such situations may be akin to Freire's (2000) banking concept of mechanistic, dehumanising education. In the banking concept, students are empty containers to be filled with appropriate instructional content by teachers: 'having, rather than being is what counts', as Freire discusses in relation to Fromm's concepts of 'biophilic' (organic, living) rather than 'necrophilic' (mechanistic) personalities, applied to education (Freire, 2000:77). The banking concept of education may be effective in instrumentalist economic terms, yet is diminished by its lack of creativity and authenticity, its inability to engage with more human living values of transformational self-fulfilment. In meeting the continuous targets set in a performative banking culture of education, the power of authentic engagement in living leadership values is lost, since, as Simpson and French (2006) observe:

> The pursuit of truth has been replaced by the pursuit of targets. The principle of performativity, which pervades our culture at every level, puts pressure on organisational members – and their leaders above all – 'to subordinate knowledge and truth to the production of efficiency' (Fournier and Grey, 2000:17).... the dominant image and language of leadership focuses on this 'production of efficiency', on decisive action in the pursuit of future outcomes and goals. It is a focus that may leave too little space for the reflection that is sometimes necessary for a new thought to emerge or be found in the present moment. Those who do take 'time out' from work, to attend a course or 'away day', for example, frequently observe that the most beneficial aspect of the experience is having the time and space to do some thinking. (Simpson and French, 2006:251)

The awareness of living human values tends to encourage goals that may be less materialistic than the values of the banking concept but which are richer in understanding. Freire's problem-posing critical inquiry in education aims to effect freedom from oppression through a dialogic process of 'conscientisation', practised for the love of humanity (*ibid*). Education is not a zero-sum game of winning or losing immediate achievement targets in the longer term, but a lifelong journey. It is possible for educational goals to encompass both high standards of achievement and also deeper human understandings and values. For the achievement of wider holistic humanitarian goals in education, though, conceptions of educational leadership need to be sufficiently flexible, collaborative and multidimensional to cope with the complexity and paradoxical uncertainties of a 21st Century humane education built on shared, living, democratic values.

Karp and Helgø (2008) are amongst those theorists who consider leadership to be an emergent, interactive social process rather than a fixed phenomenon possessed by individual managerial leaders. Arguing against existing mainstream paradigms of leadership and management in their discussion on the future of leadership in an increasingly post-managerial society, Karp and Helgø (2008:33) build on complexity theory to describe leadership in organisations as a dynamic, fluid group process in which leadership is 'a shared social influence process of relating,' rather than an immovable set of authoritative characteristics of one individual or management team at the top of a positional hierarchy. In this view, leaders are influential sense-makers within an unpredictably interactive social organisational system, who acknowledge they cannot control everything, can admit ignorance when necessary and can cope with uncertainty, complexity and dynamic change.

Karp and Helgø (*ibid*:35) argue that 'taking account of relationships in the act of leading is ... better understood as leading by acting in the moment but at the same time paying attention to our experience' (*ibid*: 35). They conceive that '... organisations behave like ongoing reality construction entities – there is often no one reality leaders can decide on' (*ibid*:32). For leaders, acceptance of uncertainty and unpredictability in organisations encompasses a necessity to recognise that leadership involves an acceptance of some lack of control, while nurturing the ability of 'followers' to 'find their way to act in the moment.' (*ibid*:30).

Simpson and French (2006) are also amongst those who discuss the importance of living in the moment for leadership. They argue that leadership includes 'negative capability', the ability honestly to recognise ignorance, the state of unknowing, and the '*capacity to be available for thought* on behalf of a group or organisation, that is, to formulate 'thoughts' that are present in the emotional matrix of organisational experience' (Simpson and French, 2006:246). In this understanding of leadership, leaders need to try to discern and respond to what the social system 'needs' at the time, and to be aware that others in the organisation may be required to act as leaders. As Simpson and French note,

> ... it may not only be the designated leader who is able to think new thoughts on behalf of an organisation. Any organisational role can have a leadership dimension, which is mobilised to the extent that the role holder demonstrates this capacity to be available for thoughts that are 'around' in the system, whether as ideas or as behaviours, emotional states or other 'symptoms. (Simpson and French, 2006:248)

Moments of authentic leadership

Building on these understandings of organisational complexity and unpredictability, it becomes clearer to consider that, almost every day, there occur in organisations, small, unplanned, almost unnoticed, powerful breakthrough *moments* of authentic leadership, in which people at different levels express what is needed within the social system at the time. These moments are often informal, sometimes irreverent and startling in their suddenness, frequently taking people off guard. They seem to arise from nowhere, just as humour sometimes bursts out in a crowd when people least expect it, emerging serendipitously from an unknown source and rippling into spontaneous laughter.

Such shared leadership moments may bring us back to earth with a salutary bump when we have lost touch with mundane affairs, reminding us noisily of our common humanity. Frequently, such small, fleeting moments are not planned as part of the espoused organisational rhetoric, the longer-term 'grand narratives' of senior managers; nor are they routinely encapsulated within the strategically planned management-speak of institutions. Yet, at other times, such moments may emerge spontaneously or irreverently from the discourse and behaviour of formal leader-managers, as if to defy the logic of anti-managerialist claims that positional leaders are invariably inauthentic.

These moments are neither the property of senior/ middle management, nor of any other levels or kinds of staff. By contrast, they seem to emerge from many different people at various positional levels in different times and places, as part of the ebb and flow of the living human dialogue within organisations. Such moments are frequently overlooked and tend to remain unanalysed, being dismissed as disruptive and irrelevant. They could be considered to be the leadership equivalent of the 'atypical, noncanonical 'small' stories' (Georgakopoulou, 2004:unknown) that Olson and Craig (2009:548) describe in their accounts of the ways in which teachers and students 'live in small moments of diversity unseen and unheard within prevailing managerial meganarratives of accountability'.

These breakthrough small moments, providing authentic flashes of leadership insight, sometimes take people forward to achieve beneficial outcomes, despite barriers and tensions. Such moments of dazzling virtuoso leadership may be quixotic or comical. Sometimes they are poignant or resonate with sadness. But always they are authentic, and dance to inspire others. They can also sting, speaking truth to power with harshly accurate critique at times when others are too frightened to speak. These leadership moments occur spontaneously: the leaders enacting them may be anyone, though hardy individuals tend be the authors of such moments more than others.

This chapter analyses selected moments of what appeared to be authentic values-based leadership that emerged from data collected in interviews, surveys and focus groups with educational staff on trust and leadership in post-compulsory education. Rather than focus on individual leaders or followers, on formal leadership development, organisational systems or management hierarchies, this chapter analyses selected instances of heutagogic leadership emerging from the research.

Methodology

Selected narrative descriptions comprising moments of leadership experience emerged from data collected from 28 interviews, five surveys and five focus groups with educational staff in a series of research studies in 2006-10 on trust and leadership in post-compulsory education. An interpretative phenomenological research paradigm was followed, which included the transcription of exploratory interviews with selected participants. Interviews were UK-wide, face to face and by telephone, lasting from around fifty minutes to around three and a half hours. The researcher was curious about discovering what leadership meant to participants, facilitating a debate regarding how leadership interacted (or not) with trust in the experiential world of educational staff, and what the problems and issues were in organisations described by participants as 'low trust'. The concept of heutagogic leadership was developed to describe self-directed 'moments' of authentic leadership. A few selected examples of these are presented.

Heutagogic leadership

The concept of heutagogic leadership is built on the idea of independent self-directed learning described as heutagogy by Hase and Kenyon (2000), and discussed also by Canning (2010), amongst others. Hase and Kenyon observe that:

> Heutagogical approaches to education and training emphasise: the humanness in human resources; the worth of self; capability; a systems approach that recognises the system-environment interface; and learning as opposed to teaching. Heutagogy addresses issues about human adaptation as we enter the new millennium. (Hase and Kenyon, 2000:online)

The concept of heutagogic leadership is put forward as a new theoretical model that may improve understandings about the development of trust in educational leadership. The model is based on the concept of independent, self-directed, honest and authentic expressions of leadership that exist at all levels in organisations. Recognising the complex, unpredictable nature of 21st Century organisational systems, heutagogic leadership emphasises the responsibility of everyone in the workplace to develop some level of leadership in their role. The concept is values-based in mature, democratic understandings of human worth that place importance on individual 'self-determined' trustworthy expressions of shared leadership as part of a collaborative process in which participants at many levels are engaged. Heutatogic leadership is inimical to the banking concept of education, stressing independence and freedom in organisations for engagement in dialogue and critical analysis. The concept is explored further below in which moments of and about leadership were drawn from the research data.

Sting like a bee: Leadership moments captured in survey responses

Moments in which respondents' words about leadership stung like a bee in reply to the question: '*I would describe the leadership and management of the organisation I work for in the following way*' included data from Respondent 141, who 'strongly disagreed' that s/he might rate senior managers in their organisation as effective.

Respondent 41 said, bleakly, 'We work in a dictatorship with a demagogue at its helm'. This critical expression of dissatisfaction was the final comment left by the respondent, who then exited the survey. His word demagogue may give a sense of a manipulative, deceitful leader of a mob-like group of followers. The metaphor of the helm controlled by a navigational leader who heads up the dictatorship of this educational institution suggests a dysfunctional organisation in which controlling power is wielded ruthlessly by an autocratic manager. The critique is sharply judgemental, suggesting the writer might have an awareness of what could be done to improve conditions, but there is no indication of whether the respondent's reply reflected any actual engagement in leadership critique in the workplace.

In response to the same survey question, Respondent 79 also 'strongly disagreed' that they might rate senior managers in their organisation as effective, saying:

> They are arrogant, dishonest, are prepared to lead by deception. They show little interest in what we do and as long as there are no problems then they are content. Lip service only is given to any support or direction that we require. It's an *'I'm alright, Jack, sod you!'* from low to high level management, and, for that matter, also [from] the administration staff!

This sharply critical description of the leadership and management of the organisation draws attention to significant failures in the vision, culture, values, human relations and management support for staff in the college. A lack of care for and interest in staff exists at every level of the organisation, in the view of the respondent, and is further compounded by the conceited and deceitful nature of the management. There is no indication that the thought leadership of this criticism was verbalised within the college, however.

In response to the same survey question, Respondent 24 was another who 'strongly disagreed' that they might rate senior managers in their organisation as effective, saying:

> I would describe the management as completely lacking in respect for staff. It is the most miserable place I have ever had the misfortune to work in.

This stinging critique concisely sums up the respondents' perception of problems with leadership and management: a total lack of respect for staff is combined with an unhappy workforce situation, and the respondent regrets their 'misfortune' in working there. Again, no indication emerged from the survey of whether the respondent intervened to improve the situation, but the critique provides an authentic reflection, which, if shared openly, might provide leadership to others in demonstrating what might need to change.

The survey data is littered with 100+ 'momentary' responses of this nature, instantaneous expressions of critique, appreciation, concern and other reflective comments about leadership in post-compulsory education. The selections above were from low levels of trust situations that generated stinging criticism amongst respondents, but others in the survey were strongly appreciative of good leadership and management, as well as high levels of trust and openness in their organisations.

Dance like a butterfly: Moments captured in leadership interview responses

The Case of Lydia

Lydia is a senior leader employed in a national capacity who was interviewed about leadership in post-compulsory education. The interview explored the way in which a self-defining leadership moment had occurred in which she experienced a turning point in relations with a difficult group of staff. She had learnt, in her words, how 'to be authentic and vulnerable' as a leader:

> *Interviewer*: That position that you were in at Crimson College, can I just ask you about that stage in your career? What was, if you like, the turning point?
>
> *Lydia*: It was learning to be authentic and vulnerable, while also being competent and adding value. That was the really big lesson there. Because I was still coming at 'management' and all that, a lot from my head as well, do you know what I mean? I didn't feel such an experienced practitioner and – there was a lot of mistrust when I went there, because I was a young woman and they were all men in their forties and fifties. And there was this woman in her early

thirties came along (and I looked younger...). So it was sort of, '*What can she tell us?*'They'd all got MBAs – and I was terrified. I was thinking they'd all be these strategic thinkers and all of that so...

But what I learnt was that, by being really honest, really being clear and having a vision that I shared with them, and really knowing what I was doing as well. But the big turning point – and this was true at Green College as well – when I went there, was that I made a couple of mistakes early on. And I went out and I publicly apologised and explained how we'd got there. They weren't massive blunders or anything, they were about – one was about trying to reduce course hours quicker than they were ready for it – and they were up in arms. Now, I'd do it much more incrementally, but it was like, '*Come in, let's do that, got to make my mark*'. And going out and then actually saying to them, '*Hang on, I think I got this wrong, let me talk you through where I was coming from. The way I saw it was this. I was under these incredible pressures to try and impress you all and to...*'

And I was just really honest with them and [said]: '*Actually, I'm changing my decision on that now, I'm publicly acknowledging that, I've listened to what's been said, I've heard, so we're going to change that and I just hope you can hear that in the spirit it that it's given. Now if I make a mistake every day, then I think I should resign, but ...*'

... It wasn't easy – it was hard. It's being very authentic. And I discovered that at Green College. My experience is that, if you do that very honestly, it's amazing. It's almost like people *want the leader not to be perfect*, either, do you know what I mean? I mean, you can't set that up, actually, you can't kind of go, '*I'll make a couple of mistakes and I'll go and apologise, then they're all trust me or whatever*'. But they were very real. I mean, I'm like agonising over this and losing sleep and, '*What do I do with this?*'

And now, I'd like have much more courage through experience, that actually the more open you are ... and you show that. It's a form of – it's not weakness you're showing – it's vulnerability and I think it's different. But it took me a while to understand what that difference is. Those were the turning points. Do you see what I mean?

[Interview with Lydia; Jameson 2006]

The Case of James

James was a senior leader at the time of the interview, employed as the head of an institution. The interview explored a self-defining leadership moment from some years previously. He had experienced a turning point in relations with a difficult group of students and staff, risking public humiliation in front of cynics to express his belief in the students:

> *Interviewer*: You were telling me about Bruner and how people can get 'lost at sea and drown' [metaphorically, in education].
>
> *James*: And learning is like that. Now, when people feel they're drowning, that's where the good teacher needs to come in and pick them up, or else ... they drop out. I mean, why do people drop out? They actually drop out because they feel that they're not coping. So yes, part of the vision thing is understanding what is the right thing to do in those circumstances – and then the management bit is OK, well, doing them the right way.
>
> Then I went to be principal of a sixth form college in ... Yellow area ... a Roman Catholic college. And we had a lot of youngsters from a neighbouring city area. And ... that was January 1986 ... in October 1985, we'd had the riots nearby in that city.... So those youngsters ... in this Catholic college, youngsters of all faiths, it was wonderful, vibrant. When I first went, it was sort of depressed and had recently had a poor inspection. But I was thirty five and sort of a bit unaware of, you know, tail wagging, I thought, you know, '*sort this*'.
>
> But didn't realise quite how depressed the place was, and students were not liked. They were not cherished, they were ... the college would be patrolled at lunch time, people would be thrown out, and just, I mean, I felt uncomfortable. And I was the head! I mean, it's true. So you think well, the kids must, what do the students think about this? So then, that was about transformational leadership. And we spent a long time where I then tried to interpret ...Yellow area in the context of loving these kids. Some of them looked a bit frightening really, they ... But it was about transforming that institution so that everybody felt valued, you know, not just the white Catholics.
>
> And we did it, really. It was sort of long and hard, but we did it, and it was about, it was about expressing belief in the children, in the young people. And there was, you know, how through life you get significant moments? I mean, you know, in the conversion so to

speak, of that college, from being a place of depression to a place of excitement, really. We opened up areas for students so they could work there at lunchtime. And the chap leading design, opened up the design area so the youngsters could go in and work at lunchtime. It was great. And he went for a cup of coffee. And he came back and the colour printer, this was 1988, 1989, that sort of time, the colour printer had been stolen, you know, in ten minutes it was gone. Now, we only had one colour printer in the whole college at the time, because you know there weren't many computers then. We had a computer and a colour printer and someone had pinched the bloody thing! So Fred came across to me and said, 'They've taken the blasted printer!'

And so you think, '*What do you do, is this about doing the right thing? What do you do, do you ignore it?*' We didn't have enough money to buy another one.... So we, in [a systematic way] ... responded ... where you call the whole college together, you know, ring the fire alarm, [and get everyone] gathered in the sports hall.

And I stood on a table and said, '*Look, you know, we've got a problem, because somebody's pinched the printer, the colour printer from design*', and I said, '*This is so serious, really, because what it means is, that no-one...., maybe one person can use it now, at home, and nobody else can, and we sort of need it, and we can't buy another one because we haven't got the money, so look, if someone's made a mistake, we all make mistakes, but can we have it back, please?*' That's all.

So I got off the table and walked out. And there were these staff who were sort of hostile really and I walked past and you could hear them saying, '*Bloody fool!*' you know. So then you get back to your office and you think, '*Oh bloody fool, why did I do that?*' You just think, '*Oh God!*'

Anyway, ... two days later I got in and the caretaker came with a printer, and he said, '*This was on the doorstep this morning*'. So they'd brought it back. And, come the next college meeting, I just said '*Thank you*', you know. But, I sort of marked that moment as [being one which showed that] the cynics had done their bit, they'd all sort of laughed, but, actually, it worked.

And that was about just ... expressing belief in the kids that they would actually do the right thing. And so yeah, I mean, now ... it was high risk strategy, bloody high risk, because, if it didn't work, then I'm the one who's made to look a fool in front of not only colleagues but the whole school, all the students as well, you know, so, that's about... that's ...to risk, which I probably hadn't thought through, but actually it was just about belief in the kids.

There's a brilliant example of that really in, did you see *Ahead of the Class* with Julie Walters? It was, it's the film ... of Marie Stubbs' transformation of St George's School in London where Philip Lawrence was murdered. Marie Stubbs has written a book called *Ahead of the Class*. It was a fictionalisation... of reality. But what she took to the school, which was an aggressive institution, you know, the children and the teachers were at loggerheads and it wasn't working. And what she did was to come in ... and she believed in the kids, she just believed in them. That was it. And she told them that she believed in them. And she told them that, [at] her first assembly, where, you know, they were all a bit antagonistic. And then she said [to this boy], '*Look, who does this school belong to, you know, you, who does this school belong to?*' And she walked out and he said, '*Who?*' because everybody was then looking at him, 'The Pope?' (It's a Catholic school) '*The Pope?*' She said, '*No, it belongs to you, you know. And the reason that I'm here and the teachers are here, everybody's here, the bricks are here, is because of you. That's it. You're not here because of the school, the school's here because of you*'.

And it is about turning things around, you know, to get people to understand, you know, to reflect. So here [in this college], for example, I say that.... I say, '*Look, you know, the college, I'm here, not because I've got a job and you happen to come, but I'm here, if you weren't here, I wouldn't have a job, that's it, so none of us, teachers, you know, we're only here because of you*'. And some of the teachers feel a bit uncomfortable about that, but it's true. It's exactly what it is.... And sometimes it's just telling people explicitly, well, with vision I suppose, that's what it is. It's saying, '*Look, this is it.*'.... Because you know ... in a sense, what people are looking for is *understanding*.

[Interview with James; Jameson 2006]

The case of Deirdre

At the time of the interview about leadership, Deirdre was a team leader in a college who had just been made redundant. The interview explored the way she had acted as a leader to create openness and trust with her team and other managers, while coping with a situation in which she had been made redundant as a result of minor mistakes which could have been corrected:

> *Interviewer*: What kinds of leadership behaviours do you think have built trust?
>
> *Deidre*: Well, I would have said that *openness...* you know ... to give you a for instance, I had a report from another group – another area in the college – that my area was perceived to be ... various negative things. So I was just given this as a piece of bald reporting that had gone to my Director, and she said, '*You know, look, there's these five areas where they think that [your team] is not performing.*' So I made an appointment to go to the group that had made this report to speak to them about what it was that we weren't serving them in, and how to correct it – and, before I went – because it would have been a week before I could go – I said to my own team, '*I've had this report: I'm going to investigate it and I wanted you to be aware of it, that if somebody comes in, sort of thing, into the office and is funny with you, that that's where it's come from.*' So I felt they needed the information in order to do their jobs well.
>
> However, my Director felt that I shouldn't have shared it with them, because they were sort of too low level and they didn't need to know it, and all it did was make them unhappy. My reasons for doing it were because I wanted them to be aware that there was an issue and to just be that bit more sensitive. So in that situation, I felt that they needed knowledge, which my superior thought that they didn't. But I don't feel you can keep people in the dark, because otherwise the situation can compound. And that was my view from my experience and her view from her experience was different. In the event, most of the things that I found that were issues could very easily be cleared up and very few of them had substance, but the level at which they'd complained was quite serious....
>
> Would you like to know about the redundancies? ...Well... I was told I was going up for a meeting ... so I went and I'd done reports ... and I took it all up and I sat there with my huge pile of stuff. And they said, '*There's no easy way to say this, but you're going to be made redundant*'. And that was a terrific shock. It was the stuff that heart attacks are made of. And I said that in the meeting. I stood up and identified myself, because the other thing was that nobody knew who the others were – there were rumours and counter-rumours – so I identified myself in the management meeting and, sure enough, the other seven managers that were affected – well .... ten managers,

because there are eleven of us – came up and identified themselves to me, as a result of that. But, at the time I stood up and said, '*Look, you know, it should have been done by an announcement on the Monday that said, 'Because we have problems with – you know, whatever it is they've got problems with – we will be making people redundant, this is only going to affect 70 individuals and eventually we will only lose 21 individual people, but if you are in the frame you will be informed by Friday*". Which would have meant one week of uncertainty. Instead of which all of us that were told, had a terrific shock.

They then sent an email around to everybody on the Wednesday, telling everybody there were redundancies going on, but not who it was. Email! ... you know, there were some people not in the know at all. Nobody had spotted it, so nobody had said, 'Hang on a minute, we've missed this very important, crucial announcement hasn't been made to all of our staff, some of whom were affected. And also some people hadn't individually been told that they were being made redundant. There was one I know of, off sick, who wasn't informed and got the email about – talking about the redundancies – including, obviously, her! – she hadn't been told. So – it was just completely botched. The trust level is rock bottom.

[Interview with Deidre; Jameson and Andrews 2008]

The case of Alison

Interviewer: ... What do you feel about the level of trust between the government and/or regional sector managers and your institution?

Alison: One of [the] things I come up against when I'm talking to lecturers is that we're supposed to be run as a business, but .... we're not really a business... what they're saying is that their college ... has just run up a bill of debts of £10m, £100m ... and it's just got to a state of collapse. It's not like [a business]. They would disappear. ...Everybody on the senior management team would lose their job ... everything would go, and there would be a hole in the market, and you would have to go to somewhere else for your knickers, or whatever it is being sold.

When a college goes bust, all that happens is that the senior staff change and the logo changes. So how can this drive to business actually be honest? It's a fabrication, it's a pseudo state of affairs ... because, being in business means ... you don't only take the profits, but ...you take the pain. Now ... you cannot close down FE colleges,

> because you have got a whole swathe of unemployed youth from ...14-19 that you cannot just dump in the streets. You've got to put them somewhere...
>
> If there was a bit more honesty about the fact that they are trying to hide this problem of this great big swathe of socially-excluded youngsters ... maybe if there was some honesty about that, maybe some of the problems ... inherent in that deceit would allow [us] to be able to work out what was going on. It's a fundamental deceit. The basic deceit is that it is not a business. It's a social exclusion unit, or something. You can't close down hospitals [or] ... schools when they go bust. You cannot close down the FE sector, in somewhere like a major city with its ten colleges because it's running at a loss. What would you do with the hundreds of thousands of teenagers? There has to be some honesty. It's a euphemism. There will never be a problem about educating the top 20 per cent of the population. Educating the bottom 80 per cent is a problem that has never been resolved. We're still dealing with that.
>
> [Interview with Alison; Jameson and Andrews 2008]

Conclusion

The small stories of informal authentic breakthrough leadership moments described here 'dance like a butterfly, sting like a bee', in that they express levels of honesty, openness and trust in taking a risk about telling the truth as the perceiver sees it. Such moments occur every day in organisations at all hierarchical levels. They can support colleagues to sustain their trust in organisations and to achieve beneficial outcomes, despite barriers and tensions. Moments of dazzling virtuoso leadership, sometimes humorous, sometimes poignant, always authentic, dance to inspire others, as in James's story. They also sting, as do the respondents' words from the survey reported above, speaking truth to power with harshly accurate critique.

The concept of heutagogic leadership was developed to capture a way of theorising and understanding the self-directed moments of authentic leadership that came to light spontaneously during the course of this research, when participants demonstrated independent evidence of their view that 'everyone in the workplace should be their own leader'. The heutagogic leadership model may prove useful in improving understandings about the development of trust in post-compulsory educational leadership.

References

Canning, N (2010) Playing with heutagogy: exploring strategies to empower mature learners in higher education. *Journal of Further and Higher Education* 34(1) p59 -71

Freire, P (2000) *Pedagogy of the Oppressed.* London: Continuum International Publishing

Georgakopoulou, A (2004). Narrative analysis workshop: How to work with narrative data. Paper presented at Narrative Matters 2004: An Interdisciplinary Conference on Narrative Perspectives, Approaches, and Issues across the Humanities and Social Sciences, May, 2004, Fredericton, New Brunswick, Canada

Hase, S and Kenyon, C 2000 From andragogy to heutagogy. ultiBASE publication by Southern Cross University.: http://ultibase.rmit.edu.au/Articles/dec00/hase2.htm (accessed 28 November, 2010)

Jameson, J (2006) *Leadership in Post-Compulsory Education: Inspiring leaders of the future.* London: David Fulton/Routledge Education

Jameson, J and Andrews, M (2008) *Trust and Leadership in the Learning and Skills Sector.* Research Report. Lancaster University: Centre for Excellence in Leadership

Karp, T and Helgø, T (2008) 'The future of leadership: the art of leading people in a 'post-managerial' environment'. *Foresight* 10 (2) p30-37

Olson, MR and Craig, CJ (2009) Small Stories and Meganarratives: Accountability in Balance. *Teachers College Record* 111(2) p547-572

Simpson, P and French, R (2006) Negative Capability and the Capacity to Think in the Present Moment: Some implications for leadership practice. *Leadership* 2 (2) p245-255

Acknowledgements

Grateful thanks to all interviewees, institutions, recent and prior survey respondents and focus group members participating in leadership research. Thanks also to the University of Greenwich for internal REF funding, to the Centre for Excellence in Leadership (CEL)/ Learning and Skills Improvement Service (LSIS), Inspire Learning and the University of Lancaster for funding for research in previous years. Thanks to Dr Margaret Andrewsfor co-researcher support on the 2007-08 CEL Trust and Leadership project. A few short paragraphs from respondents are reproduced from Jameson (2006) and Jameson and Andrews (2008), within the new context of this reflective article.

PART TWO: EDUCATION, TRUTHS AND VALUES

5

Becoming a European Citizen: Education to Overcome Mistrust

SIEGLINDE WEYRINGER

The establishment and nurture of a European identity is one of the main aims and challenges for the European Commission and for the European Parliament. The ideal is that each citizen in any member-state of the European Union should integrate in his or her general self-consciousness a sense of belonging to this supranational community. The idea has many roots and origins. For instance, there is the desire to overcome the historical legacy of wars between member states, and it is the case that the present experience of globalisation seems to necessitate an economic union based not only on material values but also on ethical ones too. This latter intention is not new since Jan Amos Comenius and Immanuel Kant anticipated the idea of the European Union in their work many years before its establishment.

This idea is now being realised with the EU Commission providing the essential institutional structures and the financial base. My interest lies in investigating the conditions and correlations necessary for success, with a particular focus on what is needed for the development of people who are able to function and live well within the new global world and yet who retain their awareness of their social and national backgrounds.

One of the most ambitious goals of the European Union is to inculcate a sense of European citizenship in all who live in member countries. The idea of a European citizenship is based on a concept which acknowledges the centrality of both diversity and equality. As well as a lack of a precise definition or description of what constitutes and characterises 'the ideal European citizen', mistrust of other national groups is one of the main obstacles to the realisation of this concept. Mistrust has its origins in personal experience and also in the collective memories of national communities and it affects and has implications for various aspects of social life.

The EU government has initiated many educational programmes designed to develop a sense of European citizenship. The evaluation of these programmes reports encouraging effects, especially with regard to the numbers of young people applying to and participating in them. The question is whether the enhancement of mobility and activity resulting from these projects is sufficient to create a social climate of trust and tolerance, because these attitudes are part of the self-concept and the constitution of personal individuality. The obvious answer is no and this chapter will highlight findings which support this assessment. The way forward, therefore, is to devise educational programmes which combine knowledge about issues related to the European Union with the development of personality components and values education.

Platon Youth Forum, an international summer campus for gifted young adolescents, is one such programme which uses a specific didactical approach, 'VaKE' (Values *and* Knowledge Education), aimed at developing a sense of European citizenship. The approach concentrates on strengthening personal abilities to cope with cultural diversity and on developing a stable self-concept integrating knowledge and the values-ladenness of actions. This chapter describes the programme, the didactical approach and also discusses findings of an evaluation investigating the effects of participation on selected aspects of knowledge and personality.

From an educational perspective, the establishment of trust seems to be a crucial element if the desired positive effects are to be achieved. Trust in individuals and trust in institutions is regarded as the essential foundation for the establishment of European identity. This chapter investigates this assumption, analyses necessary conditions for the establishment of trust, and presents an educational programme aimed at overcoming mistrust developed over centuries between the European nations.

The idea of European citizenship

The government of the European Union has put many efforts into educational programmes aiming to promote and to embed the idea of European citizenship in the consciousness of its inhabitants. The notion of European citizenship was introduced by the Treaty of Maastricht (1992) and further developed by the Constitutional Treaty of Lisbon (2007) and focuses on individuals who are citizens of one of the member-states of the European Union but who also acknowledge and embrace an identity as European Citizens.

The concept of European identity is based on the idea of shared values related to human dignity, freedom, fairness, tolerance, equality and solidarity as well as to principles of democracy and the rule of law. All attempts to establish this identity place the individual at the heart of their activities. Three main strategies are followed with the aim of realising this citizenship-ideal: (1) to disseminate information about European institutions and to enhance the communication about European topics in general; (2) to inform the citizens about their rights; (3) to inform the citizens about their duties, especially those concerning their active participation in creating the European identity.

Since 1992 the European Commission has been putting this idea into practice, developing and organising a variety of educational programmes for all ages and interest groups of European citizens. All activities of the Lifelong Learning Programme focus on the realisation of the European integration process not only by law but also through seeking to influence the minds and feelings of the European citizens. The goal is to create a European society.

In 2004 the European Council implemented the programme *Active European Citizenship* with the following objectives: (a) to promote and disseminate the values and objectives of the European Union; (b) to bring citizens closer to the European Union and its institutions, and to encourage them to engage more frequently with its institutions; (c) to involve citizens closely in reflection and discussion around the construction of the European Union; (d) to intensify links and exchanges between citizens from the countries participating in the programme, notably by the way of town-twinning arrangements; (e) to stimulate initiatives by bodies engaged in the promotion of active and participatory citizenship. The programme takes the form of four strands:

Active Citizens for Europe; Active Civil Society in Europe; Together for Europe; and Active European Remembrance. These strands support the activities of civil society bodies and other structures such as municipalities and organisations of such bodies working at European level in the field of active citizenship (European Council, 2004).

2005 was declared as the Year of European Citizenship through Education. In this year the programme *Youth in Action* concentrated its funding on projects with relevant objectives. EACEA, the Education, Audivisual and Culture Executive Agency, was founded in 2006 to manage the Lifelong Learning Programme and furthermore to create and realise additional ideas and programmes promoting European citizenship education. The goal is to increase and strengthen the perception of the European Union as a societal community which goes beyond economic alliances.

The level of interest and participation in all the activities mentioned would seem to suggest that these programmes are likely to have a positive effect on individual awareness of Europe as a social as well as an economic union. However, the feeling of belonging to a community or being a member of a society can't be enacted by legislation or governments. Psychological as well as sociological processes and dynamics are involved and therefore have to be considered, if the idea of European citizenship is to stand a chance of realisation. Thus I will now move on to discuss psychological and sociological components and their interactions as these are relevant to the establishment and nurture of citizenship awareness.

Identity as a precondition of citizenship

All theoretical and practical approaches to the conceptualisation and understanding of identity and citizenship centre on the Kantian questions 'Who am I?' and 'What should I do?' The construction of personal identity follows developmental processes integrating cognition, affects, emotions and mentality, and it takes place in interactions between the individual and the environment. These interactions can either support or perturb the established personal self-concept of an individual person. Piaget (1977) formulated the theory according to which the development of cognitive structures depends on whether an experience can be assimilated into one's existing cognitive structures, or whether these structures have to be accommodated in such a way that the particular experience can be integrated. If none of these two adaptive processes is practicable, the specific interaction between a person and the environment wouldn't be registered and recognised and, furthermore, wouldn't have the potential to become a personal experience. A personal experience is, according to this theory, determined by emotional and cognitive arousals, and has a supportive effect on the development of mental aspects of personality (Kegan, 1982).

If these interactions are recognised as problems and conflicts, an intensive stimulus on the development of personality could be anticipated (Erikson, 1959; Marcia, 1966). A disequilibrium of the existing cognitive structures (*sensu* Piaget) or a cognitive crisis (*sensu* Marcia) can be a consequence, caused by either an inner personal conflict between mental conditions or between the differing possibilities an individual sees as being available, or by an interpersonal conflict between the standpoints of different people. If the end outcome of a crisis leads to an inner commitment made to a certain role or value, the person has reached the status of a well-developed identity and has a sense of their strengths, weaknesses, and individual uniqueness. These findings have relevance for citizenship education. Activating emotions effects coping strategies for the cognitive challenges inherent in problem solving processes, and the realisation of meaningfulness and self-efficacy indicate crucial criterions for personal active participation in a democratic civic society.

Especially during adolescence the process of shaping and stabilisation of individual identity is the main developmental task for an individual (Havighurst, 1948; Erikson, 1968; Marcia, 1980). Young adolescents could, therefore, be a main target group for citizenship education.

Sociological analyses of the development of identity concentrate on the interaction processes. The term 'the looking-glass-self' (Cooley, 1902) is a metaphor for the relationship between the individual and the society. The individual recognises himself or herself in how others react to what they do. However recognition alone isn't sufficient for the growth of self-concept. Self-reflection is also necessary in order to integrate experiences with other persons into the developing identity. This reflective thinking includes the interpretation of the other person's reactions and understandings as well as an assessment and a judgement of the whole interaction. However, this process can lead to misunderstanding and misinterpretation, and therefore it needs evaluation. A communicative exchange between the interacting partners, and finally a recheck during further similar activities and situations in the future have to take place. Following Mead (1934), this evaluation of experience will make apparent whether there exists congruency between the individual's self interests (I), uniqueness and anticipatory orientation, and the individual's self awareness of the expectations and the society (me), represented by expectations and reflexive orientations of significant others.

Brewer and Gardner (2004) point out cross cultural studies that have suggested that the personal self can be conceptualised in two different ways: either as individuated or as interpersonal. The first concentrates on the priority of individual interests and egoistic motives, whereas the interpersonal conceptualisation focuses on the relationship of the individual with other persons. However, these different self-constructs may also coexist and be available within one individual person. Both are aspects of the personal identity.

But how does the individual self become a social self?

Personal identity means the development of the individual self as well as of the social self. The more these two parts of the self-concept are integrated within each other, the more stable and reliable is the construction of an individual's identity. Cooley (1902:209) has interpreted the group-self meaning we as an I that includes other persons.

The social self is determined by concepts of meaning, cultural values and the orientation towards past, present and future within a society. It can be developed as soon as an individual has gained the abilities to reflect on one's self, to take the perspective of another person and to act from this position (Selman, 1980). Mead (1934) found that a child learns this perspective-taking in doing role-plays and imitating people with whom they have an intimate relationship. In these role-plays the child learns to understand and to anticipate the thoughts, the way of thinking, the emotions and feelings these people have in specific situations. The child imitates parents, friends and other people to whom they are close in their habitual performance of acting, talking, discussing and solving problems. Based on these experiences and knowledge, the child continues to learn about the acting, talking and feelings of other people.

Playing games within a group or participating in competitions, the child becomes aware that membership in a group provides benefits in many aspects of life and personal concerns which are based on the tenets of mutuality, reciprocity and responsibility. The experience and knowledge gained by group-membership can be formulated with the slogan 'I have to give before I get'. This means active participation and contribution are the first step in order to enjoy the rewards of the fulfilled expectations. The child learns that group-membership is combined with expectations on him or her defined by the role and position they hold within the group. On the other hand, they realise that other people share the same interests, motives and values and, further, that belonging to a group can reduce problems – because they are shared – and can widen horizons by bringing additional and better goals and objectives into the personal focus.

Being an accepted member of a group contributes in many ways to the construction and constitution of identity. The *me* aspect is strengthened by the feedback of the group, how well the member fulfils their role, and meets expectations. The *I* aspect of identity can grow because the individual realises achievability of previously unachievable goals and interests. This analysis of the impact of group membership on the development of identity fails to account for critical awareness of the goals and values orientation held by a group. This is significant because individual decisions to apply for membership are influenced by personal appraisal of the dominant values orientation in the group. However, my view is that the mechanism of establishing cohesion and obligation within any group works more or less in the described manner above, independent of the values orientation of any particular group.

With regard to the social or interpersonal aspects of personal identity, an additional distinction has to be made: that is, the quality of relationships between group members. A group member can establish a closer relationship to another group member or subset within the group. These intimate, dyadic and small group interactions mould the prototype of interpersonal identity established. In contrast, collective identities aren't grounded in personalised relationships; they derive from the perception of sharing the same values and belonging to the same social category like a profession or a nation. Additionally, collective identities are influenced by the conscious recognition that there are outsiders who don't share the same values hierarchy or the traditions, life-styles and knowledge as do members of the established group. Emphasising the difference between insiders and outsiders strengthens the solidarity between the group members (Elias and Scotson, 1965).

Despite this differentiation of the self-concept at the personal level, there exists a basic orientation within a society concerning the quality and the extension of bonding between the individuals. This orientation forms the image of a national society, indicated as the culture or mentality of a nation. Mentality as a characteristic of culture can be defined as a system of values and ideas, morals and customs, a set of conventions that control the social institutions and determine the functions and meanings of the artefacts of a group or society (Posner, 1991: 122). Symbols support the sense and experience of belonging to a group. Group symbols aren't limited to graphs, pictures or signs; they include behaviour, dress-code, preferences and language. All these components together create an image people have of individuals belonging to a specific group.

Language becomes a symbol of this belonging, because members of a group tend to create a special use of words to express their shared understanding and points of view, ie the language of young adolescents. Language is never private and is always a social phenomenon characteristic of a group (Wittgenstein, 1953). Using the same language is a reference to a shared cultural tradition of understanding based on the same experience within an environment. In addition to Posner (1991) and following Lewis (1969), the term 'mentality' can also be explicated semiotically as sets of conventions, ie preferred responses for problems of coordination in cooperative action and communication, and the control of these responses. On the other hand, language is a representative tool fostering the mentality in a group or in a society. Mead (1934:132) defines mentality as the ability of the organism '... to point out meanings to others and to oneself'. Telling stories and narratives essentially supports the adjustment of the individual personality towards the predominant mentality and fosters the establishment of collective identity (Czarniawska, 2004).

Comparable with the development of the individual self, the genesis of a social self depends on interpretation, judgement and the communication of relevant events recognised as important by the majority of members of a community. The more a person involves themself in issues important for the further existence of the community and participates in discussions and problem solving processes, the more they become aware of personal strengths and weakness, and of the effectiveness of behaving in particular ways. The constitution of identity is the product of these social activities. Problems and conflicts can lead to stronger identities, especially when the person is able to cope with the challenges associated with the process of solving the problems.

The background of these processes is formed by the mentality of a group or of a society and its basic orientation towards individualism or collectivism. Hence, the individual shapes society, and society shapes the individual, so neither the individual nor society can be separated from each other. To create the consciousness of *We* on the level of groups, the collective self-concept has to be developed based on the establishment of the individual-personal and the social-interpersonal self-concept.

Postmodern concepts of identity claim multiplicity (Keupp *et al*, 2002) and impermanence, suggesting that identity is never fixed but remains fluid and in a perpetual state of flux. These theoretical concepts receive support from new communication technologies which have opened up access to information from all over the globe. This access to knowledge and experience involves responsibility for actions and enables the engagement of the individual in a dimension that has never existed before. Anyone who wants information about a specific issue can usually find out all (and more) they need to know by accessing the extensive resources available via the worldwide web. The media provides up to date news and real time information about occurrences all over the globe.

As a consequence of open access to information, it is less easy for people to claim ignorance or to fail to find out the information necessary to enable them to understand how to solve many of the problems that are frequently encountered. This access to knowledge has implications for identity construction: for any actions and decisions of everyday life the individual could, more or less, take global consequences into account. Nowadays a person can often decide for themself the extent to which they want to be informed. The information is available; the common argument for refusing commitment, 'I didn't know because of lack of knowledge', has turned into a weak one.

Another challenge is the possibility of creating very individualised and autonomous life-styles, putting previous traditions into question. Research on processes of problem solving suggests that a rise in the number of possibilities increases the complexity of a problem, and as a consequence complicates processes of decision making and solution finding (Doerner, 1979). This societal change entails the loss of certainty and reliability in the appraisal of expectations, interactions and their consequences. The situation can affect the development of identity in a negative way, and, as a consequence, can inhibit the capability and motivation for active participation in civic society. The individual is confronted with a paradoxical situation: the increase of hypothetical possibilities might reduce the real possibilities of a person finding what the best way of life is for them, because of the impossibility of investigating the viability of all of the possibilities. The new argument for refusing commitment and participation can be formulated as 'I don´t know what to do because of lack of parameters for critical verification of possibilities'.

Regarding the matter of European citizenship, this paradox can particularly confront adolescents who are already potentially experiencing identity uncertainty, with additional difficulties. First, the question 'Who am I?' has to be differentiated according to a variety of reference groups, for example 'Who am I as a unique individual, or as a member of a group, or as a citizen of a nation, or as a citizen of the European Union?' Second, for all these different domains of personality, a huge variety of answers can be found. Each answer increases the possibilities of deciding what an individual should do. All answers and decisions on actions should have the potential to be integrated in a general consciousness of authenticity in all situations of participation. Coping strategies, therefore, need to reduce this complexity. One of these coping strategies is the establishment of trust in relationships (Luhmann, 1973) and the next part of the chapter concentrates on the relationship between trust, identity and citizenship.

Trust as a precondition of identity and citizenship

Trust between individuals, and between individuals and institutions, is the main keystone for the functioning of a society. No legislature and no government have the potential to replace trust between its citizens with regulations and laws. Gambetta (2000:217) has defined trust as

'... a particular level of the subjective probability with which an agent assesses that another agent or group of agents will perform a particular action, both before he can monitor such action (or independently of his capacity ever to be able to monitor it) and in a context in which it affects his own action'. This definition integrates the main components of the phenomenon and makes its complexity obvious: subjective hypothesis of a probability, subjective assessment of an action, uncertainty, risk, impossibility of satisfying control and influence, and forward focusing.

Trust is combined with the expectation of reliable adherence to given promises and agreements (Rotter, 1980). Reciprocity, development over time and limitation to specific domains characterise a trustful relationship between individuals or between an individual and a group or an institution (Schweer, 1996). The aspect of reciprocity emphasises the relationship between the partners of trustworthy interactions: both are involved in the exchange of giving and taking trust, and in the adaption of personal interests and expectations. Trust depends on a developmental process of growth, which has to be gone through with any new relationship and with any new area of interest. Having trust can become a general and relatively stable attitude of a person (Rotter, 1980).

The establishment of trust is the fundamental step of psychosocial development during the lifespan; the stability of the personal self-concept depends on self-confidence and self-trust (Erikson, 1959). Therefore, self-confidence and self-trust are preconditions of the construction of trust in others, because these two components give the ability to an individual to cope and to overcome frustration in cases of disappointment. Trust can be, and has been, more generally defined as a device for coping with the freedom of others, because the agents are given a degree of freedom to disappoint the expectations of each other (Luhmann, 1979).

The aspect of freedom concerning assessment and choice of possibilities to act is a crucial factor for trustworthy relationships between agents. On one side, trustworthiness increases the possibilities and autonomy for their actions and decisions, so that trust becomes a mechanism to reduce the complexity of societal reality (Luhmann, 1973). On the other, the confidence in trustworthiness limits freedom for those to whom is given trust, because they are expected to behave in a special way.

Trust between agents can be developed in three phases: (1) implementation of a trustworthy communication, (2) phasing-out of threatening actions, (3) targeted development of trust (Petermann, 1996). This model induces a step-by-step process including verbal and non-verbal signals of willingness of open-mindedness, understanding, activity, giving attention, support and feedback, self-disclosure, emotions, empathy, tolerance and respect, giving freedom and autonomy. It includes the readiness to discuss issues and topics, which might provoke criticism, judgement and rejection.

This model of trust-development has relevance for face-to-face relationships. The constitution and establishment of trust in and within a social group with a huge number of members needs additional procedures based on the agreement of the community that their use will establish trust. This trust in the function of procedures, like the use of money, the establishment of institutional authorities and the implementation of government based on the rule of law, is a main requirement for the development of modern societies (Simmel, 1923; Luhmann, 1973). The quality of trust-development essentially determines the success of the cooperation between different societies, nations and cultures. The challenge of the genesis of trust between these groups can be detected in the fact that the interactions are carried out by individuals, who act as representatives of an institution, of an organisation or of a network belonging to such a group. Trust-development is modulated by the consistent interdependence of personal points of view and public opinion of the represented group.

Trust in international and intercultural networks and organisations is generated in a very slow evolutionary process running through three phases based on calculated self-interests, on knowledge about each other, and on identification of shared values (Lewicki and Bunker, 1996). Especially at the start-up phase, self-interests are likely to dominate the motivation for the relationship. Therefore, the interactions between the partners have to be approached very carefully, because even a single event has the power to destroy confidence in the trustworthiness of the partner-organisation (Lo, 2004). The establishment of trust between different organisations and networks needs a stable and advancing progress based on activities and interactions being acknowledged as consistent and coherent towards the interests in question.

The quality of communication determines the second phase. Depending on the frankness with which the parties speak about their needs, preferences and problem-solving strategies, they give each other the base for understanding, for the establishment of appropriate expectations and for the motivation to stick to the given promises. Joint experience and permanent and repeated interactions give the opportunity to get to know these motives, interests, ways of thinking, values orientation and preferred strategies of problem-solving. Primarily, such events have a formal character. A strong network of informal, interpersonal relationships supports this process, because through these relationships the partners can achieve a greater mutual knowledge, and they can nurture their ability to predict each other's strategies (Mutti, 1990).

Trust produced by institutional arrangements cannot replace trust based on the integrity of individual actors. If the institutional framework for trust is incomplete and instable, personal trust does not only supply, but even replaces this framework (Welter *et al*, 2004). Trust in and between persons, institutions and organisations is based on individual persons and their experience with each other.

The reality of trust in the European Union

Since 1973, the Eurobarometer, an instrument to survey public opinions on central issues related to the European Union and European integration, has provided periodical reports. These reports include questions concerning the confidence of individuals in European and national institutions, and also questions concerning European identity. The survey EB 70 (European Parliament, 2009) sought views on the trustworthiness of various institutions. Part D of this survey focuses on confidence in European and international institutions. The participants were asked how much they tend to trust several institutions. The results report that the participants of this survey put the European Parliament at the top (51% of the citizen tend to trust this institution), followed by the European Central Bank (48%), the European Commission (47%) and the European Council (42%).

In contrast to these results, the survey reports a tendency not to trust national institutions (for National Parliaments 58%, for National Governments 61%). So it can be said that the confidence in European institutions is higher than in national equivalents. Compared to former surveys, trust in European Union institutions remains more or less the same. Hence, an increase in the share of respondents that do not trust each of the four main institutions has to be mentioned. For the European Parliament the distrust increased from 27 per cent to 31 per cent. The European Central Bank rated the largest increase of distrust (from 24% to 30%).

In this survey, respondents were also asked which elements would most strengthen their feeling about being a European citizen. Most of all (39%), a European social welfare system harmonised between the member-states would support this feeling. The youngest citizens (15 to 24 years old) give a special importance to a European ID card in addition to a national one. In general, European identity is shaped by the currency, the Euro (40%), democratic values (37%), history (24%), the success of the European economy (23%), culture (22%), the European flag (15%) and the European Union's slogan 'Unity in Diversity' (12%). Concerning the progress of European integration, 56 per cent of the citizens think that the European Union has grown too rapidly. Nevertheless, 54 per cent agree that building the European Union must be pursued. Only 18 per cent want a European civic education for children from primary school age on.

Concerning the growth of European identity-consciousness, these data are drawing a picture that doesn't evoke a storm of enthusiasm about the success and the effectiveness of all the established programmes. In this regard, the outcomes are humble compared to the financial investment. (The budget for Lifelong Learning Programme 2007-2013 is nearly E7 billion.)

This fact might be a consequence of problems of organisation, management and communication. Hence, these causes touch only the surface of the problem. I would suggest that the main reasons for low trust in the European Union can be found in the historical experience the European nations have with each other, combined with national historiography and the tradition of history lessons in schools. General knowledge about historical events in Europe can be simplified in categories of war and conquest. National interpretations and assessments of this sort of interaction have influenced national concepts of identity. Negative mental attitudes and prejudices towards other nations have been fostered in many ways, ie with xenophobic jokes, with the reduction of access to information and by featuring the idea of supremacy and hegemony in many aspects of social life. All these combine to create an emotional gap between countries and societies intended to strengthen the cohesion and solidarity within the national society.

Additionally, the national dominance of political orientation influences public opinion in a civic society concerning social openness or exclusion towards groups identified as others. Political elections and ruling parties very often foment existing prejudices and fears against cultural and ethnic minorities in order to win votes. Such campaigns are based on the assumption that the citizens are not informed or do not have an interest in challenging the proposed image of the others. Austria provides an example of the use of these problematic strategies when, in the autumn 2010 election campaign, a right wing party sought control of the City Council of Vienna.

After using such strategies, the ruling parties have to fulfil the expectations of their voters in order to maintain power and influence as soon as the election is finished. One possible strategy is to strengthen the produced image of the others and to act according to the expectations of the voters using all instruments and structures of legislation and government as well as putting influence on media and public communication. How should a critical citizen react, knowing that it is probably a ploy? Refusal to participate in elections is one possibility; another one is to withdraw trust in political institutions. Neither possibility supports the nurture of a stable identity because they lack the sense of belonging to a reliable community far in excess of personal relationships.

Other obstacles for the idea of European citizenship

In Europe different national orientations towards citizenship and national identity have grown over time. The member-states of the European Union also have had different experiences with democratic procedures. For instance, citizens in South-East European member-states experienced totalitarian regimes over centuries, first under the authority of the Ottoman sultanate and afterwards during communist dictatorship. Although overcoming these autocratic systems of governance was achieved through the shared motivation and will of the citizens, this fact doesn't automatically entail the ability to deal with democratic structures and with possibilities for creating and participating in active citizenship-initiatives. Primarily, the citizens of these nations had, or still have, to develop their own novel vision of national identity and citizenship. So the idea of European citizenship might be an excessive demand for nations with emerging democratic practice.

The citizens in the EU member-states west of the previous Iron Curtain also show difficulties and problems in establishing a vision of European citizenship, which is practicable in everyday life as an integrated part of self-concept and identity. Despite the existence of the legal base, the theoretical discourse concerning the question, which identity this concept produces in contrast to the national identity-concept, is still without a final answer (Lehning, 1999; Déloye, 2000; Dobson, 2006). The slogan of the European Union doesn't facilitate the problem of clarifying the idea of European citizenship, because it cannot be supposed that the citizens have a practical understanding of it.

Regarding the elements constituting identity-based citizenship, a lack of basic definitions and the clear operationalisation of their meaning in everyday life can be identified. This assumption concerns (a) the precise description of the habitus of the ideal European citizen ('Who and how am I being a European citizen?' How do I act and feel being an European citizen?'), (b) the precise geographical description of Europe regarding the idea of European citizenship (all European countries or member states of the European Union?), (c) the clear statement concerning the constitution of the European Union (unity of nations or united states?), (d) the clear description of rights and commitments an individual has being a European citizen in comparison to national citizenship, (e) a clarification of the relationship between the government of the European Union and the national government concerning autonomy within membership and participation, (f) the knowledge about the cultures integrated in this community, (g) the competences dealing with diversity concerning language, culture, ritual acts of communication and strategies of problem-solving, (h) the positive remembrance of joined experiences, (i) the knowledge of the European constitutional tenets, (j) the knowledge and understanding of the interference of European and national constitutional rights and duties.

All these elements can be seen to have an important impact on the development of interpersonal or social aspects of identity. Therefore, educational efforts to overcome the paucity of clarified meaning have to concentrate on the nurture of the practicability of the European citizenship idea at the personal level of the self-concept.

Platon Youth Forum: Education for strengthening European identity

Platon Youth Forum is an international summer camp for gifted young adolescents coming from all member-states of the European Union as well as from other countries. This programme has been organised by ECHA-Austria (European Council for High Ability – Austria) and the University of Salzburg, Department of Education since 2004. The aim of the Forum is to promote European identity and citizenship according to the paths and objectives of the European Union explicated above. The participants are invited to work on current European problems for one week, taking into account the different national perspectives and focusing on historical and cultural differences of understanding and interpretation. Five workshops are offered; the teams in each workshop are multinational.

The issues for discussion focus on the discourse of solidarity with respect to autonomy and on the identification of social injustice and inequality in Europe, for example: energy supply (Nabucco pipeline); society and the money economy (investment banking); solidarity during times of financial crisis (insolvency of a nation); the need for and the worth of expensive research (national financial support of CERN – European Laboratory for Particle Physics); hierarchy of responsibility in a political system (court case on firing order at the Inner German border between the Federal Republic of Germany and the German Democratic Republic); personal responsibility (question of free will), and the justification of becoming involved in other nations' wars (Afghanistan and Iraq). The challenge is to elaborate the problems from the perspective of a hypothetical person, who has to make a decision on what to do. This decision has to be defended during discussion.

The discussion of these problems is very complex due to the integration of a very personal point of view with standpoints on a national level and on the level of the European Union. The educational goal is: the individual participant should have positive experiences in solving complex problems with respect for and tolerance of opposite points of view and in working towards an agreed solution. This solution should maintain the differences of argumentation based on the individual's personal hierarchy of values and principles as well as on the national preferences of judgement and assessment of the participants' mother countries.

A specific didactical approach, VaKE (Values *and* Knowledge Education) has been developed to provide an appropriate teaching algorithm for reaching this ambitious goal (Patry, Weyringer and Weinberger, 2007; Weyringer and Patry, 2007; Weyringer, 2008). This approach is based on the principles of constructivism *sensu* Piaget (1951), Glasersfeld (1987) and Foerster (1984), and it integrates investigations on moral judgement (Kohlberg, 1981) and studies on dilemma discussions (Blatt and Kohlberg, 1975). The prototypical course is organised in eleven to sixteen steps, and it incorporates phases of exploration, decision making, research, discussion and personal reflection on the process of solving the identified problems. The procedure is initiated by personalised dilemma stories. The characteristic of these stories is an incongruity of ethical values and principles. The protagonist is exposed to a cognitive and ethical conflict, and he or she has to decide what to do. The question 'What should I do in the role of the protagonist?' is central to all the dilemma stories.

Independently of a particular decision, the problem cannot be solved without harming an ethical principle fundamental to the personal self-concept. Several mutually excluding options for decisions are proposed; each option is connected with a specific values orientation. The individuals can choose between agreement and disagreement with the proposed action, or they can abstain from voting. In any case they have to find arguments for their personal decisions during the following debate. During the defence of their individual points of view, they are likely to realise that they lack knowledge to strengthen their arguments. So they have to investigate relevant facts and information, either by contacting experts or by using libraries and the internet. The gained additional knowledge is shared with all participants to provide an equal basis for the following consideration of the decision. The individual participants have the option to revise their previous standpoint but have to be able to give good reasons for changing their opinion.

The discussions as well as the search for information provide profound challenges in undertaking a viability-check concerning individual knowledge bases, the level of the ability to make moral judgements and with reference to preferred individual values. This check makes apparent whether the acquired knowledge as well as the personal values hierarchy, on which the decision is based, could lead to a viable possible solution of the problems in question. Several phases of reflection provide time to reorganise the mental and emotional balance.

The participants can also be given the challenge of defending the opposite point of view. This task enables them to comprehend the motivational, affective and cognitive constitution of the contradicting party.

The process is brought to a tentative end when a shared solution, which acknowledges the dissents manifested in the discussions, is proposed. Several feedback-loops, called Forum, are implemented in the programme: the other workshop groups form the audience of the first Forum; the second audience is composed of persons who have real expertise in the addressed issues. Both audiences give feedback as to whether the proposed hypothetical problem-solutions are likely to be viable in reality.

Several cognitive, affective and pro-social abilities can be set into practice, for example: critical thinking; role-taking; empathy; coping with multilingual conversation; control of and coping with affective and emotional arousal during discussion; self-regulated knowledge acquisition; sensibility of the values-loadedness of problems and for the diversity of values and principles; creating novel approaches for dealing with complex problems.

From 2004 to 2007 an evaluation of the programme took place. The research was designed as a pre- post- follow-up inquiry combined with daily inquiries during the workshops. Several questionnaires were developed focusing on a variety of hypothetical constructs related to components of personal self-concept and identity. Besides other investigations, the study summarises the answers of these questionnaires given by 180 young adolescents coming from fourteen EU-member states who have participated in workshops held over the past 4 years.

The results show a significant increase of components related to interest in and awareness of the personal values orientation as well as a significant increase of self-confidence in the stability of this aspect of identity within the week that the Forum takes place. These effects seem likely to have their roots in the elaboration of the proposed dilemmas as well as in the informal interactions during leisure-time. The participants developed a clear sense of tenets constituting ethical behaviour; ethical values became more important for their decision-making; they developed a more informed and critical vision of right and wrong; they increased their sensitivity to the consequences at stake; in making decisions they orientated themselves closer to justice, to role-models and towards their own preferred values and principles; they attributed themselves with having strengthened their ethical self-concept by developing more empathy, tolerance and understanding for opposite standpoints; they experienced the ability to develop and change their self-consciousness; they became more aware of the responsibility for this change being on themselves, not on others.

Regression analysis showed that the enhancement of these aspects is caused by the level of emotional and affective involvement in the problem solving process. Cognitive factors, like critical thinking and the viability check of knowledge during the debates, seemed to have no impact on these developmental processes. Concerning the question of which orientations and references influence the decision, a significant decrease of the orientation towards the reference-group can be reported. At the end of the week the participants demonstrated a higher autonomy towards their friends and towards group-pressure.

All these effects are long lasting. Follow-up studies undertaken each year, nine months after the Platon Youth Forum, indicated that participation in this programme has initiated a steady interest in issues and problems of the European Union, a higher sensitivity for the diversity of problems and possible points-of-view, a stronger self-confidence in personal abilities of problem-solving and discursive discussions of complex problems. The participants experienced new strategies to follow their personal interests with respect for and taking into account the interests of counterparts. Working on current European problems in a discursive manner has provided an environment in which the adolescents have established durable friendships. They have gained personal experiences which challenge existing historical traditions. (Weyringer, 2008)

Synthesis

Based on these findings, Platon Youth Forum can be described as a civic education course for young people. The following synthesis wants to put forward evidence that this event can contribute to the realisation of the idea of European citizenship, and especially to the establishment of trust between young citizens:

A communicative exchange on critical and crucial questions takes place. The interacting partners, initially perceived as outsiders, become significant others. They experience belonging to a group (the workshop-group as well as Platon Youth Forum as a group) by sharing the same values and interests (issues with European concern). This belonging is based on the challenge to work out the differences of standpoints caused by personal values priorities and the social and national background of the participants.

They realise that the discourse does not aim to reach consensus on answering the question 'What should I do?', rather it aims at the critical investigation of possible points of view. They also realise that belonging to the group previously is not dependent on approval of majority opinion, but on the level of autonomy of thinking and arguing a participant can establish during the process of investigating the problem. They learn to defend their standpoints using strong arguments; they also learn to change their minds on the basis of better verified facts, and to control their emotions during these processes. They take part in role-plays, in which they have to defend opposing standpoints or to present a viewpoint they don't agree with to an audience.

There is a competition between the workshops for the most interesting presentation. They get feedback within the group and also from the other groups and from experts. They have to organise relevant facts and knowledge for the defence of their personal point of view. They have to check whether the information is trustworthy. They have to find coalitions of mind to support the discussion. They experience unity beyond the barrier of language and beyond the dissent of culture and tradition.

The concept of the Platon Youth Forum strengthens identity, because the development is initiated by a problem, which causes a cognitive and an emotional conflict, and because the problem-solution depends on the development of coping-strategies regarding multiplicity and diversity. The voting and the argumentation during the discussions challenge the viability-check of preferred values and available knowledge. The event enhances the establishment of durable friendships and networks. This fact is an indicator that trust as a result of cooperation (Gambetta, 2000) could be established on a wider scale. The programme provides a satisfying environment to create a personal role-model of a European citizen; it has the potential to contribute to the establishment of European identity.

Finally

This chapter represents a rapprochement to the topic of European citizenship from the perspective of education, especially how the establishment and nurture of trust can support the implementation of this citizenship idea, and which educational practices can be recommended to have positive effects on this intended educational goal. Investigation of these questions draws on philosophical, psychological and sociological research and findings. With respect to this wide theoretical field, the chapter can only claim to identify and define some of the relevant components related to European citizenship education. With respect to the novelty of this issue, the transfer of existing knowledge of education as it is done in this article is problematic; the empirical base of the argumentation especially needs to be improved. Further investigations and studies in the context of education are essential, because the idea of European citizenship will continue to affect the development of personal identity as well as national education policy.

References

Blatt, M and Kohlberg, L (1975) The effects of classroom moral discussion upon children's level of moral judgement. *Journal of Moral Education*. 4 (2) p129-161

Brewer, M B and Gardner, W (2004) Who is this 'we'? Levels of collective identity and self-representation. In Hatch, MJ and Schultz, M (eds) *Organizational Identity. A reader.* Oxford: Oxford University Press

Czarniawska, B (2004) Narratives of individual and organisational identities. In Hatch, MJ and Schultz, M (eds) *Organizational Identity. A reader*. Oxford: Oxford University Press

Cooley, AJ (1902) *Human nature and the social order.* New York: Charles Scribner's Sons

Déloye, Y (2000) *Exploring the Concept of European Citizenship. A socio-historical approach*. http://scpo.univ-paris1.fr/fichiers/Yaerbook.pdf. (accessed 15th May 2010)

Dobson, L (2006) *Supranational citizenship*. Manchester: Manchester University Press

Doerner, D (1979) *Problemlösen als Informationsverarbeitung*. Stuttgart: Kohlhammer

Elias, N and Scotson, JL (1965) *The Established and the Outsiders*. London: Frank Cass and Co

Erikson, EH (1959) *Identity and the Life Cycle*. New York: International Universities Press

Erikson, EH (1968) *Identity, youth and crisis*. New York. Norton

European Council (2004) Basic Act 'Active European Citizenship'. Official Journal of the European Union. http://eacea.ec.europa.eu/citizenship/documents/legalbasis/legalbasis_en.pdf (accessed 15th May 2010)

European Parliament (2009) *European elections 2009*. Standard Eurobarometer (EB 70) – Autumn 2008. First results: European average and major national trends. http://ec.europa.eu/public_opinion/archives/ebs/ebs_303_brut_en.pdf (accessed 15th May 2010)

Foerster, H von (1984) On constructing a reality. In: Watzlawick, P (ed) *The Invented Reality*. New York: WW Norton

Gambetta, D (2000) Can we trust trust? In Gambetta, D (ed) *Trust: Making and breaking cooperative relations*. Electronic edition Department of Sociology, University of Oxford. http://www.sociology.ox.ac.uk/papers/gambetta213-237.pdf. (accessed 15th May 2010)

Glasersfeld, E von (1987) *The Construction of Knowledge. Contributions to conceptual semantics*. Salinas, CA: Intersystems Publications

Havighurst, RJ (1948) *Developmental Tasks and Education*. New York: Longman Inc

Kegan, R (1982) *The Evolving Self*. Cambridge, Mass.: Harvard University Press

Keupp, H, Ahbe, T, Gmür, W, Höfer, R, Kraus, W, Mitzscherlich, B and Straus, F (2002) *Identitätskonstruktionen. Das patchwork der identitäten in der spätmoderne*. Hamburg: Rowohlt

Kohlberg, L (1981) *Essays on Moral Development, Vol. I: The philosophy of moral development*. San Francisco, CA: Harper and Row

Lehning, PB (1999) *European Citizenship: Towards a European identity?* http://uw-madison-ces.org/files/lehning.pdf. (accessed 15th May 2010)

Lewicki, R and Bunker, BB (1996) Development and maintaining trust in work relationships. In Kramer, R andTyler, T (eds) *Trust in Organisations. Frontiers of theory and research*. Thousand Oaks CA: Sage

Lewis, D (1969) *Convention. A philosophical study*. Cambridge, MA: Harvard University Press

Lo, V (2004) Vertrauen in dienstleistungsnetzwerken des finanzsektors. In Mayer, J (ed) *Vertrauen und Marktwirtschaft. Die bedeutung von vertrauen beim aufbau marktwirtschaftlicher strukturen in Osteuropa*. http://www.forost.lmu.de/fo_library/forost_Arbeitspapier_22.pdf. (accessed 15th May 2010)

Luhmann, N (1973) *Vertrauen. Ein mechanismus der reduktion sozialer komplexität*. Stuttgart: Ferdinand Enke

Luhmann, N (1979) *Trust and Power*. Chichester: Wiley

Marcia, JE (1966) Development and validation of ego identity status. *Journal of Personality and Social Psychology*, 3, p551-558

Marcia, JE (1980) Identity in adolescence. In Adelson, J (ed) *Handbook of Adolescent Psychology*. New York: Wiley

Mead, GH (1934) *Mind, Self and Society. From the perspective of a social behaviorist*. Chicago: University of Chicago Press

Mutti, A (1990) The role of trust in political exchange. In Marin, B (ed). *Generalized Political Exchange. Antagonistic cooperation and integrated policy circuits*. Frankfurt: Campus

Patry, JL, Weyringer, S and Weinberger, A (2007) Combining values and knowledge education. In Aspin, D and Chapman, J (eds). *Values Education and Lifelong Learning* New York: Springer Press

Petermann, F (1996) *Psychologie des Vertrauens*. Göttingen: Hogrefe

Piaget, J (1951) *The Psychology of Intelligence*. London: Routledge and Kegan Paul

Piaget, J (1977) *The Development of Thought. Equilibration of cognitive structures*. New York: Viking Press

Posner, R (1991) Society, civilization, mentality: Prolegomena to a language policy for Europe. In Coulmas, F (ed) *A Language Policy for the European Community. Prospects and quandries*. Berlin: Mouton de Gruyter.

Rotter, JB (1967) A new scale for the measurement of interpersonal trust. *Journal of Personality*. 35 (4) p651-665

Rotter, JB (1980) Interpersonal trust, trustworthiness, and gullibility. *American Psychologist*. 35 (1) p1-7

Schweer, M (1996) *Vertrauen in pädagogischen Beziehungen*. Bern: Huber

Selman, RL (1980) *The growth of interpersonal understanding*. New York: Academic Press

Simmel, G (1923) *Soziologie. Untersuchungen über die Formen der Vergesellschaftung*. München, Leipzig: Ducker and Humbolt

Welter, F, Kautonien, T and Stoytcheva, M (2004). Trust in enterprise development, business relationship and business environments. In Höhmann, HH and Welter, F (eds) *Entrepreneurial Strategies and Trust. Structure and evolution of entrepreneurial behavioural patterns in 'low trust' and 'high trust' environments of East and West Europe. Part 1: A review*. http://www.forost.lmu.de/fo_library/forost_Arbeitspapier_22.pdf. (accessed 17th May 2010)

Weyringer, S (2008) VaKE in einem internationalen Sommercampus für (hoch)begabte Jugendliche. Unpublished dissertation. University of Salzburg

Weyringer, S and Patry, JL (2007) VaKE and education for leadership and European citizenship. *Journal of high abilities*, 12 (14) p4-27

Wittgenstein, L (1953) *Philosophical Investigations*. London: Blackwell Publishing

6

Becoming a European Union citizen – getting to the end of the highway to heaven

KAMILA KAMIŃSKA

The systematic transformation that started in 1989 brought two major changes to Poland and other countries of the post-soviet region: one was the sudden availability of toilet paper; the other was the closure of soviet military bases and the departure of that foreign army from the country. Joining the European Union in 2004 was perceived by the majority as the most natural second step on the highway to the heaven of the Western part of the world; it also put an end to hundreds and thousands of Polish citizens being sent back to the country while trying to cross UK borders each month (some only as tourists) and made it possible for over 250,000 to get legal jobs there, a fact that might not be perceived in the same, positive way by UK citizens as it is by Poles.

This chapter explores some of the aspects of these two processes analysed from an educational perspective. A brief presentation of the political and social transformation that has taken place over the last twenty years gives the context for deliberations on some of the paradoxes emerging from it. The chapter looks at the growth of different forces of resistance towards power that led Poland to overcome totalitarian Communistic rule and that then somehow disappeared in the face of the neoliberalist new world. This is shown to be a very complex pedagogical situation.

Any presumption that after the Communist regime fell there was an automatic return to an idealised Polish culture is naive optimism, which brings with it a great variety of educational challenges. A possible fruitful recourse for answers is found in the field of critical pedagogy, especially in the writings of Freire (2009), hooks (1994, 2009) and Szkudlarek (1993) together with the Polish traditions of resistance through street art, proposing paradox, the palimpsest and the absurd as pedagogical concepts.

Towards the highway to heaven

Eastern Europe, especially Poland, has always been aware of its vulnerable geopolitical position. Being stuck between Germany and Russia was never easy. As the Ukrainian writers, Andruchowicz and Stasiuk, state:

> Being put between Russia and Germany is a historical destination for Eastern Europe. Eastern European fear is historically balanced between two fears: the Germans are coming; the Russians are coming. For Eastern Europeans death is always a prison or extermination camp death; and it is sure to be a mass death: massenmord, zaczistka. For Eastern Europeans travel is always an escape. But to and from where? From Russians to Germans? From Germans to Russians? It is so good that in situations such as these the world still has America. (Andruchowicz and Stasiuk, 2007:46)

I am convinced that not only our place in space but also our place in time is unenviable. While Western European thinkers working in the field of critical pedagogy feel no ambivalence in their critique of capitalism or neoliberalism, citing Marx or even Mao (Freire, 2009:94), they are in the comfortable position of not having experienced Communism in practice as we did for fifty grey, poor and often violent years in Eastern Europe. Belonging personally to the generation that experienced all three periods: Communism, the transformation and the era after joining the European Union, I feel an awful reluctance to respond enthusiastically to those Western prophets of revolution. I feel really unfortunate and hopeless.

Polish history is full of heroes fighting for freedom (from France to America and back home), and is marked by new beginnings. We regained our freedom at least twice: once after almost 200 years of civic resistance and acts of revolution against three states who shared our territory, and again after World War II. Our literature is a record of the nation's dreams of a better world. We have a special experience here of using Fukuyama's (1992) concept of 'the end of history': the history of dreaming ended as the final dream came true. During the fifty years of the Communist regime, Polish citizens were cut off from Western Europe, crossing the border was strictly controlled and getting a passport was an amazing privilege reserved for the chosen few. The grey and sad reality of what we experienced every day was in sharp contrast to those visions from the West that were somehow smuggled to us. Kapplani (2009:5) describes a 'borderline syndrome' with symptoms such as irrational fear and restlessness while crossing the border.

Probably the best picture of the state of mind associated with Polish migration and Communism is the movie *300 Miles to Heaven* directed by Maciej Dejczer, released in 2001. It is based on the true story of the two Zielinski brothers (15 and 13 years old at the time) who were so determined to escape Communist Poland that they hid under a truck and in that way made their way to Denmark (in reality it was to Sweden) (Fleming, 2007). After a 300 mile journey they were finally discovered. The audience in the cinema hold their breath for a moment as a little boy with great big blue eyes asks the most important question of his life: 'Are you absolutely sure it is *Capitalism*?'

Borderline syndrome may serve as a much better tool for understanding the Polish eagerness to join the European Union than some of the more sophisticated narratives of political scientists such as Berezin (2009), who uses two explanatory dimensions, the strength of the state and the strength of the nation, for her analysis. Her conclusion is that the Eastern European states (including Poland) are weak and therefore easily gave up their sovereignty to the European Union. The notion of an imperialistic Poland 'from one sea to the other' (the Baltic Sea to the Black Sea) is to be rejected; nevertheless it is clear from Polish history and from everyday life in Poland that such a thesis about Poland is rather risky. Poland's first king, Boleslaw Chrobry, was crowned in 1025; the oldest text in the Polish language dates back to1270 CE.

Another powerful moment in *300 Miles to Heaven* shows the two teenage boys walking the streets of Copenhagen which are decorated for Christmas and staring at the store's windows full of all sorts of goods. They truly feel they have got to heaven. One needs to experience the lack of literally anything in the shops (with one silly tin of sardines keeping its position on the shelf) to understand their amazement. It is not only Western thinkers who have a problem with visualising this astonishment; the younger generation in Poland do not understand this either.

It is easy to criticise Eastern European's love for MacDonald's, Coca Cola and Levi's jeans. It takes a little more effort to bear in mind that before 1989 the only people who wore jeans got them smuggled from Turkey, that Coke had its ugly Polish replacement and that the dream of every child was of chewing gum with a picture of Donald Duck on the wrapper that was only available if you could pay with dollars in PEWEX stores. In the light of the 6.2 per cent growth in the economy in 2006 and 6.5 per cent in 2007, Poland has been proclaimed a 'tiger' of Eastern Europe. Voices such as Hardy's (2009), critical of our optimism regarding the spectacular success of capitalism, sounded hopelessly pessimistic when presented at conferences, and were dismissed by readers of the book.

The Polish economy does look gleaming on the surface: there are great shopping malls, glass skyscrapers in Warsaw and expensive cars on the streets. The beneficiaries of these changes are represented in the media and in mainstream city images; those who paid too high a price for the so called 'shock therapy' to the economy after Communism are heavily burdened with the stigma of unemployment and poverty and are therefore invisible (Hardy, 2009:10-12). Perhaps this is why probably the most interesting book on the Polish transformation was written by the American political scientist, David Ost. His main argument could not have been expressed by an insider:

> Post-Communists set in motion the articulation of class differences that the political world was unable to process as such, due to both structural legacies and current ideological fashions. As a result, emerging class conflicts became articulated not as conflicts over interests but as conflicts about identity. (Ost, 2005:179)

Ost's questions have their interest. But more typical of eastern European questions are those such as: 'Was he or she a Communist secret agent? A cooperator? Is he a true Pole or post-soviet garbage?' The Czech Republic opened their Communist archives just after 1989. This resulted in dramatic and traumatic shock therapy. People discovered that their friends, spouses or priests had been collaborating with the Communist regime, so that, maybe because of them, individuals were sent to jail or even sentenced to death. The story of Poland's agents is not finished yet, with shocking information coming out now and again (especially around election periods) about important people whom Polish citizens trusted; an example is the accusations against Lech Walesa. Twenty years after the fall of Communism we have not resolved these identity conflicts.

In 2004 another significant Eastern European movie was released: *Czech Dream* (Klusák and Remunda, 2004). The plot concerns two students from the Czech Film Academy who commission a leading advertising agency to organise a huge campaign for the opening of a new supermarket named Czech Dream. The supermarket, however, does not exist. The documentary reaches its climax at the opening of the store where we watch masses of people storming the fake door.

The movie has been described by the *Variety* journalist Eddie Cockrell (2004, online) as 'an original, cheeky treatise on capitalism, with more than a whiff of exploitation' and by the *Economist* as 'probably the funniest European film of the year' (*ibid*). Watching the movie, I did not laugh once. It left me sad; and angry towards the sophisticated anti-consumerist young directors who made monsters and idiots of the ordinary people shown in the movie, most of whom, as was made clear from their appearance and language, came from disadvantaged backgrounds. Their vision of happiness was not perhaps the most poetic, nor acceptable to critical intellectuals; but it was a vision based on a real experience of need very different to what the directors have known themselves. The movie makers did not impress with their smart demystification of the manipulating power of advertising and their condescending mockery of the blinding power of consumerist greed.

Proper critical thinking requires deeper analysis than this, recognising the basis of that Czech dream as conceptualised in the film by the shopping mall. As educationalists we must seek answers to much deeper questions: How do we show people other activities than consumption worth their engagement? How do we open their minds and hearts to values other than materialistic goods, especially when they have experienced the lack of so many things? How do we promote resistance to the rat race in nations so that people discover the value of work and the fulfilment and satisfaction that comes from that when under Communism there was almost 100 per cent employment and very little work ethic, so that not to work was sometimes a patriotic virtue?

It is easy for outsiders to criticise the way people have been blinded with consumerism here in Eastern Europe; perhaps they have never seen empty shelves in stores. It is easy for people to talk about revolution when they have never been even close to the danger of being imprisoned for their beliefs. How many left wing intellectuals in the Western world have heard of people like Popieluszko who were killed for what they taught? It was so easy to sell neoliberalism in Poland: we were all dreaming of capitalism, with childish requests to Santa to bring us oranges for Christmas. It was easy to make Polish citizens trust in the European Union – we simply did not see any other option. We might feel more attached to the Slovak soul of the Russians; but we would never trust Putin or his colleagues for our future safety. The only significant opposition in Poland to the idea of joining the European Union came from nationalists and Catholics, who were still holding on to the dream of great, mighty, self sufficient, almost imperialistic Poland.

Paradox, palimpsest and absurdity as resistant educational strategies

The metaphor of the palimpsest is widely used in postructuralist writing, being derived from; 'the image of writing on parchment, writing that was only partially erased to make way for new writing, each previous writing therefore bumping into the shaping and reading of the next layer of writing' (Davis, 2000:139). In her discussion of Othering, Atkinson writes

> My approach... involves the public confession and examination... of my own prejudices, and a thorough exploration both of how they have come to be so firmly fixed through the effects of a range of social, cultural and political discourses, and of what alternative discourses can be brought into play in order to counteract their pervasive effects. We explore the metaphor... and consider the ways in which this metaphor applies to the disjunction between my tacit and explicit beliefs. (Atkinson 2005:91)

Atkinson's account is similar to the Jewish idea of looking at ordinary things as if inscribed on a palimpsest, which has made Ashkenazi Jews seek deeper truths under the surface of reality (Heschel, 1995). An example of such a positive palimpsest is found in the work of the Orange alternative movement in Poland. After the civil war, Polish citizens were forbidden by law to express dissident political opinions;

people were sentenced to imprisonment for their political views; many were murdered. Using public spaces as agoras, people started to write liberation texts on the walls. Very quickly they were covered over with paint by the military. Most buildings on main roads soon had those ugly stains of paint on them with freedom texts just visible underneath. The Orange alternative movement then started painting dwarfs on those stains. The military regime was too serious to fight with dwarfs; they did not seem a seriously dangerous enemy. This was a huge mistake!

This is an example of the positive use of the palimpsest metaphor: liberatory texts were covered with paint; but the dwarfs rewritten on them were speaking their language, somehow releasing the message. Looking naïve and unsuspicious to the regime, they became a powerful tool in the fight for freedom.

More recently, and more disturbingly, in contemporary Poland the inscription of a Western discourse of capitalist commodification overlays earlier and more stubbornly ingrained discourses of resistance, deriving from a powerful sense of Polish national and cultural identity. As has been shown in the history of the last 70 years, Polish culture has never been easily assimilated by invading ideology. Atkinson looks at how to expose and get rid of an underlying ideology of racist and class supremacy. In the case of contemporary Polish culture, the reverse project needs to be brought forward: to recover and reaffirm cultural values and insights currently being overwritten by Western consumerism.

Poland has deep traditions of resistance through informal practices in public spaces. Apart from the serious and formal political opposition against Communism performed by Solidarnosc, there were members of Polish society, especially the younger generation, who showed resistance to state power in their use of public spaces. Art has been used as a medium for absurd and sarcastic humour to convey deep political meaning. The Orange alternative was both an artistic and a social movement. Founded by Waldemar Fydrych in 1980 in a time of civil war in Poland, it started with the painting of graffiti dwarfs. Then in 1985 it became more serious. The leader recalls: 'I thought the Militia would run after us taking hats off the people's heads. But the Militia surprised me. They instead began arresting the dwarfs.' Images of the street actions of the Orange alternative, often involving hundreds or thousands of citizens and the police, were broadcast to the whole world and became an icon of liberty (Fydrych, 2008:40).

Can this be an inspiration today? Does it have any relevance to contemporary problems? Under Communism the enemy of freedom was clearly defined. Who is it now? Street artists and graffiti writers from groups such as Kolektyf or Twożywo seem to have taken notice and have started their fight on city walls. Colonisation of public spaces has its own speed in Poland, probably the same as the growth of capitalism. Nevertheless, street art finds its way and, like the Orange Alternative during the Communist regime, continues the fight for freedom.

After the fall of Communism and the transformation that followed, there were two significant outcomes: a lack of trust towards the state and the assumption that there was no great power to resist, or to fight against. The dangers of the totalising power of commercialisation and globalisation in terms of international corporations have rarely been recognised in Poland. The younger generation seems to a large extent to have adopted the model of making money and living easy lives, perceiving education only as a tool for a career, another possession that can be bought with money and that serves only material uses. Are they truly free?

Major Waldemar Fydrych considered martial law (Communist violence) as an opportunity for the development of one's own independent reflection (Fydrych, 2008). Mezirow (1977) regarded political experience as a chance for transformative learning. Freire (2008) called for critical consciousness. An example of all these is given in street art and graffiti, which constitute contemporary arenas of free thought and serve as an impetus for reflection. Street art works as a tool of empowerment and helps to reclaim spaces that have been colonised by business corporations and state powers. Issues from gender, ethnicity and ecology to antiglobalism and class struggle are just a few areas addressed by that art, forming a free public dialogue (Ganz and Manco, 2004). Crazy art work, performed, for example, by the Barsky brothers in Sweden, encourages citizens to stop for a minute of reflection and brings back an idea of public spaces as making a city people's playground (Barsky, 2006). The founders of the Orange alternative were perceived as freaks by many; nevertheless they had a tremendous educational impact on society, giving people hope in their fight for freedom.

After the fall of Communism in Eastern Europe we lost two things: the obvious enemy and therefore the object of critique and resistance, and, maybe more dramatically, we lost the language to conceptualise goals for the future, to change the world. The amazing feeling I had at the first DPR conference came mainly from the words that I heard: of the need for change, the critique of capitalism, of class struggle and of social justice. I had not heard such a vocabulary for some time, at least not in my educational sciences context. Emancipatory pedagogy as we know it in Poland is concerned mostly with child liberation. It is true that Polish and Eastern European thinkers are slowly regaining the language. 'Political Critique' is an important think tank in our country; left wing parties have started to speak with younger and therefore different voices (for example, Piotr Żuk, 2010); nevertheless I still have a feeling that those ideas sound better in English then they do in Polish.

Looking back to the history of resistance in Poland and to one of the richest critical traditions (the Jewish one), I am meditating on new ways that, although they might not lead us on the highway to heaven nor change the whole world, might nevertheless help us to change a piece of our world, not the personal but the inter-subjective and even collective world. I have in mind such categories as paradox and the absurd and how they may appear in pedagogy.

Sainsbury offers a useful definition of paradox:

> an apparently unacceptable conclusion derived by apparently acceptable premises. Appearances have to deceive, since the acceptable cannot lead by acceptable steps to the unacceptable. So generally we have a choice: either the conclusion is not really acceptable, or else the starting point, or the reasoning has some non obvious flaw. (Sainsbury, 1995:1)

Clark (2007) points out that although most paradoxes are fun to deal with they are also serious. They provoke critical thinking by the very fact that they show gaps in our way of perceiving, understanding and defining reality. For example: Solidarity was a working class movement with support from intellectuals, artists and students but Solidarity's victory over Communism became its people's defeat. It seems that what paradox and palimpsest have in common is that they are both examples of ways of thinking that challenge our too easy understanding. In the case of the palimpsest, the older ideas are overlaid with newer ones; in the case of paradox, the ideas are in collision and seemingly irreconcilable. Critical thinkers in Poland have to say yes to the freedom from Communism; but also yes to the continuation of critique. We are reminded of Oscar Wilde's: 'I can resist anything except temptation' (Wilde, 1893:11) when contemporary thinkers and practitioners appear to be saying: 'I can judge from anywhere except from where I am standing.' What we all need is a standpoint from which to evaluate: where can we stand, apart from our culture – so as to inspect its values? There is no such place but there has to be one. That is the paradox.

Paradox reflects the fundamental complexity of human beings. Heschel (1997) claims that if we rely only on common sense we do not notice paradoxes around us; he argues that we need to lean upon reality, look deeper into our world of experience and not ignore the paradoxical, as by doing so we are missing the truth. This truth is the 'living truth', a blending of the universal and the individual, of idea and understanding, of distance and intimacy, the ineffable and expressible, the timeless and the temporal, body and soul, time and space (Heschel, 1997:10).

As a Jewish philosopher, Heschel easily frames his ideas in a religious discourse using religious references; but they may usefully be applied to educational theory and practice. Surrounded by the communicational chaos of contemporary times, paradox may help us to catch students' attention, rather than selling knowledge as a marketable commodity to students, in the way denounced in Freire's (2009:72) critique of 'banking education'. Appreciating the fact that there might be some deeper, hidden meaning to the obvious and the official is fundamental to critical thinking. Creating opportunities for noticing paradoxes needs dialogue as a basis for learning and living:

> I become through my relation to the Thou: as I become I, I say Thou. All real living is meeting. (Buber, 2004:17)

Absurdity

The Concise Oxford English Dictionary defines *absurd* as 'incongruous, unreasonable, ridiculous, silly'. Polish laughter at the absurdity of Communism was a source of strength and resistance. Some contemporary critical thinkers and artists use the same strategy to resist consumerism now. The film referred to above was based on the absurdity of the *Czech Dream* imaginary supermarket. The question that should be posed here is: 'whose laughter is this?' For the laughter of the outsider is patronising and misplaced; what is needed is laughter from inside the culture – which is being delivered by street art and the Orange alternative. But Communism, it seems, was a lot easier to laugh at than capitalism. What can we laugh at? Santa's big belly is not enough. Our consumerist greed, the rat race, the shrinking time for the family and the gettoisation of spaces in cities with rich and poor living separated lives may be possible objects for laughter.

Groups like Twożywo or Kolektyf are already making a powerful impact through 'education on the streets' (twozywo online). The street art of the Barsky brothers, ranging from organising a dinner in the middle of a motor way and installing swings on the city streets to painting graffiti on the snow, disrupt our everyday view of reality, and in doing so opens our minds to other spaces of knowledge and experience (Barsky, 2006).

The absurd is a category in art; but it may be worth considering from an educational perspective. We should be asking how to teach competence in reading those texts. How do we make people stop and think for a while? How do we provoke critical thought in those who are only watching now?

In the year 1986, the time of the slow but inexorable collapse of the Communist regime in Poland, I had the most significant educational experience of my life: at the age of nine I went to scout camp. Our leaders were involved in the opposition towards the regime; I was aware of this as once we all helped to display anti-Communist leaflets in the streets near my school; nevertheless I cannot recall any explicit education for liberation. Perhaps it was not safe to make overt reference in teaching to issues of liberation at a school controlled by the government; or maybe they just did not think it was a sensible thing to do with 7 to 11 year olds.

Away from school, we were in the middle of the forest, no civilisation nor culture around, only trees, our tents and the meadow with a mast and a flag on the top. The flag had four big letters displayed on it: ZSMP, which meant: Polish Socialist Youth Association. This was one of the most powerful tools used by the Communists to indoctrinate the younger generation and to prepare future party and government leaders. It was a tool that played an important role in the social life in Poland from 1957 onwards. Evidently the ZSMP had used the same camping place before we arrived.

The flag symbolised everything that the leaders of our camp hated and had fought against. Did they take it down and hide it from the children? That would have been the easiest and also the most useless thing to do. Our leaders knew there is no teaching benefit in hiding and pretending the evil things of this world did not exist; they knew that telling us a long, boring story of the history and ugliness of that Association had no value either.

What they did seems to me an ideal of critical education, of education using action, humour and the absurd to provoke thinking. They put us in formal order, little teams arm in arm standing at attention. Then the trumpet played our team's anthem and the ZSMP flag was taken down, slowly and majestically, fighting with the wind. After watching this, the teams one by one marched to the flag lying in the dust and blew their noses in it. There was no laughter; there was a crazy and absurd seriousness.

The experience reminds me again of the palimpsest: the old message of the ZSMP spoken by the regime was rewritten with a new message – the one that I blew out of my nose. Maybe it was not the most sophisticated text; nevertheless it brought a strong meaning both to the old one and to the new one being born in our young minds. This was a serious educational experience, one that taught me a profound lesson about the value of resistance. While we were blowing our noses into the Communist symbol we were learning the great lesson of education for freedom, the precious message of hope, making us feel strong and confident in relation to that dirty, ugly piece of fabric that seemed so pathetic – as did Communism for that moment.

Palimpsest, paradox and absurdity: an interesting link is the etymology of absurd – from deafness. (Surdus means deaf in Latin.) But deaf to what? We need a selective deafness: attentive to the freedom, deaf to the consumerism. But we make that discrimination from the standpoint of cultural complicity – this is the struggle that education must help us with. We need to keep on learning the art of paradoxical, absurd pedagogy and to hold on to the belief that critical thought did not die in Poland together with Communism.

References

Andruchowicz, J and Stasiuk, A (2007) *Moja Europa: Dwa eseje o Europie zwanej środkowa.* Sekowa, Poland: Black

Atkinson, E (2005) Equality, diversity and Othering: what happens to identity in a globalised world? In Satterthwaite J and Atkinson E (eds) *Discourses of Education in the Age of New Imperialism.* Stoke-on-Trent: Trentham

Berezin, M (2009) *Illiberal Politics in Neoliberal Times.* Cambridge: Cambridge University Press

Barsky brothers (2006) *Urban recreation.* Arsta: Dokument Forlag

Buber, M (2004) *I and Thou.* London: Continuum International Publishing Group

Clark, M (2007) *Paradoxes from A to Z.* New York: Routledge

Cockrell, E (2004) *Czech Dream* http://www.ceskatelevize.cz/specialy/ceskysen/en/ (accessed 15th August 2010)

Davis, B (2000) *A Body of Writing: 1990-1999.* New York: Rowman and Littlefield

Dejczer, M (2001) *300 Miles to Heaven.* Independent Artists

Fleming, L (2007) 300 miles to heaven http://www.migrantcinema.net/films/comments/211/ (accessed 9th August 2010)

Freire, P (2009) *Pedagogy of the Oppressed.* London: Continuum

Freire, P (2008) *Education for Critical Consciousness.* London: Continuum

Fukuyama, F (1992) *The End of History and the Last Man.* New York: Free Press

Fydrych, W and Misztal B (2008) *The Orange Alternative.* Warszawa: Fundacja Pomarańczowa alternatywa

Ganz, N and Manco, T (2004) *Graffiti World: Street art from five continents.* New York: Harry N. Abrams Inc

Hardy, J (2009) *Poland's New Capitalism.* London: Pluto Press

Heschel, A J (1995) *The Earth is the Lord's: The inner world of the Jew in East Europe.* Woodstock: Jewish Lights Publishing

Heschel, A J (1997) *Israel: an echo of eternity.* Woodstock: Jewish Lights Publishing

hooks, b (1994) *Teaching to Transgress: Education as the practice of freedom.* New York: Routledge

hooks, b (2009) *Teaching Critical Thinking: Practical wisdom.* New York: Routledge

Kapplani, G (2009) *A Short Border Handbook.* London: Portobello Books Ltd

Klusák, V and Remunda, F (2004) *Czech Dream.* Ceská Televize

Mezirow, J (1977) Perspectives Transformation. *Studies in adult Education* 9 (2) p153-166

Ost, D (2005) *The defeat of solidarity: Anger and politics in post communist Europe.* New York: Cornel University Press

Sainsbury, R M (1995) *Paradoxes.* Cambridge: Cambridge University Press

Szkudlarek, T (1993) *The Problem of Freedom in Postmodern Education.* London: Bergin and Garvey, Greenwood Publishing Group

twozywo http://www.twozywo.net/index.php (accessed 9th Novemcer 2010)

Wilde O (1893) *Lady Windermere's Fan: A play about a good woman.* Washington: Stationers Hall

Żuk, P (2010) The ignored reality – problems with perceiving social inequalities in the times of real capitalism: introduction. In Żuk, P (ed) *Przemilczana rzeczywistość – o problemach z dostrzeganiem nierówno´sci spolecznych w czasach realnego kapitalizmu.* Warszawa: Oficyna Naukowa

7

Trust and Rationality: Epistemic tensions in managerialism and pupil voice in schools

HOWARD GIBSON AND JO BACKUS

Introduction

There is a tension between trust and critical rationality. When we reflect upon whether we should trust, we dissolve the risk involved in trusting and trust no longer. The relationship is uneasy for, if we trust our partner, brake cable or the source of our next breath, how much potential for naivety, or worse, might such trusting bring? Conversely, since trust inherently involves risk, any attempt to eliminate the risk through rational reflection could eliminate trust at the same time (see McLeod, 2006). Thus, if trusting is risky, trust and scepticism about whom and what we should trust are in tension, and because they exist in unalloyed proximity, the epistemological unease of trust with critical rationality means that the boundary is an interesting minefield. In educational contexts, issues of asymmetry and power make the issues yet more complex. How much trust should one place in the invitation to an 'open dialogue' with a line-manager during appraisal? How much critical scepticism should a teacher engender in their pupils – to the point of nihilistic indifference or the cusp of radical action? What should you encourage, permit or require your students to trust? Later, we illustrate how this tension operates in managerialism and pupil voice, but we start by clarifying how trust and rationality are distinct but intertwined epistemic categories.

Trust and rationality

Trusting common sense is problematic. The following is an example of an ironic obituary that mourns its passing. In the appeal to its restitution, have in mind what the reader is being engendered to trust:

> *An Obituary printed in the London Times*
> Today we mourn the passing of a beloved old friend, *Common Sense*, who has been with us for many years. No one knows for sure how old he was, since his birth records were long ago lost in bureaucratic red tape. He will be remembered as having cultivated such valuable lessons as:
>
> knowing when to come in out of the rain;
> why the early bird gets the worm;
> life isn't always fair;
> and maybe it was my fault.
>
> *Common Sense* lived by simple, sound financial policies (don't spend more than you can earn) and reliable strategies (adults, not children, are in charge). His health began to deteriorate when well-intentioned but overbearing regulations were set in place...
>
> *Common Sense* lost ground when parents attacked teachers for doing the job that they themselves had failed to do in disciplining their unruly children... *Common Sense* lost the will to live as the churches became businesses; and criminals received better treatment than their victims. Common Sense took a beating when you couldn't defend yourself from a burglar in your own home and the burglar could sue you for assault.
>
> *Common Sense* finally gave up the will to live, after a woman failed to realise that a steaming cup of coffee was hot. She spilled a little in her lap, and was promptly awarded a huge settlement. *Common Sense* was preceded in death by his parents *Truth and Trust*, by his wife *Discretion*, his daughter *Responsibility*, his son Reason...
>
> (Berita Calvary, 2010)

Thomas Paine's 1776 pamphlet on *Common Sense* (1986), written following the outbreak of open hostilities between the American colonies and Great Britain in April 1775, was a polemical and tightly argued theoretical tract that bears little resemblance to what is meant by common sense in the discourse above. The spoof obituary links 'truth', 'trust' and 'reason' with what is seemingly obvious and irrefutable knowledge. It is not only gendered and intentionally un-theorised but presented in such a way that the content might equally reveal the veracity of war, the meekness of women or the naturalness of slavery. In other words, common sense is here being used as a term for a set of political, social and ethical preferences about the horrors of an over-indulgent state, family values and the benefits of discipline, self-reliance and conservative politics (see Gramsci, 1971).

The problem is that the values underlying these preferences are separated from the realm of knowledge that underpins them and, because reason is alloyed with common sense (being portrayed as his son), the depiction pays no heed to how reason might be involved in the construction of alternatives. In other words, common sense doesn't ask what *non*-common sense might be like nor whether this might be preferable knowledge, and Pring challenges the epistemic assumptions that underpin it:

> It is not clear what is this 'common sense', or how it might relate to the non-common sense knowledge of theorists and researchers. Can we identify a sufficiently distinctive area of thought that might roughly be called common sense thinking? If so, what philosophical attitude should we adopt towards it – regarding it, on the one hand, as provisional and inadequate, or, on the other, as indispensible and as the touchstone of what is real and true? (Pring, 2007:83-4)

The alternative, he suggests, is an issue of both personal disposition and epistemology. It is in part a distrustful 'manner' of looking at knowledge and received wisdom, a sense that 'one is at the beginning of the disciplined, critical and reflective thinking that is the mark of educational research'. But it is also an epistemological position that would place critical reasoning at the fore: '...a questioning and critical approach to what was accepted uncritically, a refusal to accept as self-evident what is generally believed to be true, a reflective and analytic attitude towards the fund of inherited wisdom' (*ibid*:84). In short, critical reasoning trumps common sense of which it is distrustful.

Reasoning, however, is a heterogeneous term with many meanings and functions. For Hegel it was a central tenet of dialectical progress in the 'negation of the negation' (Hegel, 1952:30), the movement from common sense, or natural consciousness, towards philosophical consciousness, on 'the pathway of *doubt*, or more precisely as the way of despair' (Hegel, 1977:49; see Tubbs, 1997:101). And this despite the confusing elevation of Reason in his latter works to a 'cunning' affinity with the inexorable progress of world history (Hegel, 1956:33). In post-modernism, reason's scepticism is fundamental to the critical, ironic detachment characteristic of its social and political commentaries that some have accused of nihilist indifference (McGuigan, 2006). And in classical liberal epistemology, despite its a-historical, culturally indifferent, individualistic rendition, critical reasoning is indistinguishable from refutation in engaged contestation. The common link here is negation.

Take Mill's *On Liberty*. Here he suggested that to exist historically means that knowledge is never complete and is inevitably partial, that to risk and test one's ideas and prejudices is a constant task and not a final solution and that the idea of truth is provisional and warranted only through argumentative discourse (Mill, 1859). For Mill it is in dialogue that contenders are forced to examine the partiality inherent in their judgements and any canonical claim to the truth such as that implied by common sense is to be understood as dogma, the antithesis of historical-discursive knowledge.

Whereas common sense finds no reason to justify its assumptions, critical reasoning finds it epistemologically essential, and whereas common sense closes its acclaimed truths to judgement, rational reflection acknowledges the tentative nature of truth itself and demands that it be open for examination. Only thus can it become grounded upon what Mill calls a 'stable foundation', something that could be trusted, for although there is no 'absolute certainty' about one's judgement there is temporary assurance sufficient for the purposes of life: 'The steady habit of correcting and completing his own opinion by collating it with those of others, so far from causing doubt and hesitation in carrying it into practice, is the only stable foundation for a just reliance on it' (*ibid*:146-7).

In short, while in liberal epistemology critical rationality involves the institutionalising of doubt through reflection which emerges as the basic precondition for improving values, theories and opinion, common sense refuses to defend its assumptions against possible alternatives and spurns a reflective and analytic attitude in favour of more sedentary, untrustworthy mental habits.

And yet. Those who explain the importance of critical reasoning also trust. They commonly trust the floor on which they stand, trust their coffee has not been spiked and trust rationality beyond all measure. Like the majority of humanity, critical reasoners are not normally tormented by or even reflective about many aspects of their daily life. Here Baier is insistent:

> We trust our enemies not to fire at us when we lay down our arms and put out a white flag. In Britain burglars and police used to trust each other not to carry deadly weapons. We often trust total strangers, such as those from whom we ask directions in foreign cities, to direct rather than misdirect us, or to tell us so if they do not know what we want to know; and we think we should do the same for those who ask the same help from us. Of course we are often disappointed, rebuffed, let down, or betrayed when we exhibit such trust in others, and we are often exploited when we show the wanted trustworthiness. We do in fact, wisely or stupidly, virtuously or viciously, show trust in a great variety of forms, and manifest a great variety of versions of trustworthiness, both with intimates and with strangers. (Baier, 1986:236)

Baier articulates mainly the physical or practical consequences of our everyday trusting but we habitually trust ideas too. While there is an obvious epistemological dilemma of invoking a return to common sense, following engaged dialogue with gainsayers the whole thrust of Mill's epistemology is that we reach a position where judgements *are* trustworthy, have *become* reliable. The aim of critical reflection in Mill is to arrive at a point of trust, however temporary, provisional or contingent this may be. Philosophers writing about the significance of testimony in trust have also argued that moral knowledge (Jones, 1999), or almost all knowledge (Webb, 1993), depends for its acquisition upon the trust of others. Others have claimed that trust is 'the very basis of morality' (Baier, 2004:180) while social theorists have extended the notion to issues of community advantage by linking 'high-trust' societies to those with high levels of 'cultural capital' (Fukuyama, 1995; Putnam, 1995; Wilkinson and Pickett, 2009).

Mathematicians and scientists also trust the testimony of other members of their epistemic communities. While there are examples where trust has been jeopardised and where the scarifying nature of reason has revealed trusting to be premature, naïve or misplaced – possibly in East Anglia University's Climatic Research Unit recently where the falsifying of evidence has been said by the press to have been 'the worst scientific scandal of our generation' (*Daily Telegraph*, 2009) –

scientists normally trust other scientists, 'unavoidably so' (Hardwig, 1991:706).

Presenting trust and reason as a dualism would seem therefore to be a distortion. In the need to institutionalise doubt there is a tension in knowing when we should postpone trust and refuse the risk involved, and acknowledging that we do trust and often put rational reflection aside. We habitually, if not constantly, trust our partners, brake cables, breathing, social mores and scientific colleagues, and this state is in tension with rational reflection upon the possibility of disloyalty, frayed wires, the telltale wheeze of the onset of asthma, or academic cheating. In other words, the epistemological interplay here of trust with distrust, of the fact that trust puts us at risk from doubt or of deference to un-argued values inherent in common sense, is evidence of an epistemological boundary in tension.

The boundary is there in Descartes (1962) where the need to institutionalise doubt resolves itself in the search for certainty against sceptical attack, doubting all until trust in knowledge is established. It is there in Hume (1973) where the solution is to portray critical rationality as 'a ship on a harbourless sea' and where trust in convention, tradition and habit is said to be the best that humans can rely upon. Put simply, if trusting is common but normal and risky, rational reflection upon whether we should be trusting is in tension with it and produces dilemmas.

So far we have suggested three things. First, that when we trust common sense we set rational reflection aside and are un-sceptical. Trusting in this way involves the risk of naivety, immorality or worse for it can embed political, social or ethical preferences that are inadequately articulated, inured from criticism and thus from the possibility of correction. Second, because of its critical, sceptical properties, critical reflection has often been seen as the Enlightenment-like solution to naïve trusting. Narratives about the negating movement of the dialectic, the critical, ironic detachment of reason, or the way truths are forced to explain themselves in argumentative discourse, are examples of how the negating power of reason has been epistemologically valued and celebrated by philosophers of different hues. Third, we have arrived at a position where the apparent dualism between the thoughtlessness of trust and the rigour of rationality is conceptually deceptive. Rationalists *trust* rationality. They also trust many aspects of their practical worlds as well as the testimony of others who dwell in their cultural, moral or scientific communities, and some have argued that this is not only unavoidable (Hardwig, 1991) but a necessity if one is to take action (Mill, 1859).

Thus a model for examining the tension between trust and rationality must account for both exigencies. One possibility is to view them as if at ends of a continuum and where *degrees* of trust and reflection go on simultaneously while living unalloyed in spacio-temporal contiguity. For example, we originally trust something, such as our brake cable, but in time may develop a rational concern. What prompts our concern is our perceptiveness or knowledge of brake cables. The growing awareness of something changing creates ambiguity. The rise of reflection through critical rationality is in inverse proportion to our diminishing level of trust, and we eventually find reason for practical action, replace the cable and so regain trust in the mechanism.

We don't remain untrusting or develop paranoia for, having dealt with the cause of our distrustfulness through critical reflection and action, we become less reflective and learn once more to trust. In a way it is an adaption of the Kuhnian (Kuhn, 1970) model for explaining paradigm shifts within science. Where unconsidered trust in a convention becomes considered, the object of developing doubt. Thus growing critical reflection then climaxes as a paradigm shift before a community of enquiry falls back to a state of temporary confidence in a set of new assumptions before the whole cycle starts again.

In the examples that follow, the chapter looks at two areas of school life and suggests that the model outlined above can provide a way of understanding the boundary between trust and rational reflection in practice. The next section looks at managerialism where it is argued that the concern for 'effectiveness', 'vision' and 'excellence' (DfES, 2004) engenders trust in instrumental or procedural equivalents that substitute inadequately for explicit values and purposes that should be rationally contested. The section following then suggests that, in pupil voice, trust is often contrived and serves purposes not revealed by those who control the discourse; that either pupils are insufficiently knowledgeable or rationally reflective to critique school policy and practice, or they are, and this jeopardises the authority of the institution that is sustained by the illusion of trust through voice.

Managerialism

Ball has argued that 'new public management' (NPM) has become 'the key mechanism in the political reform and cultural re-engineering of public sectors for the last 20 years' (Ball, 2008:47). One of the key terms in NPM has been *effective*, as in *effective* school leadership (see Reynolds and Cuttance, 1992; Teddlie and Stringfield, 1993; Teddlie and Reynolds, 2000; Blake *et al*, 1998). For some, however, the term is controversial. Bottery (2000) has suggested that effective is a word normally taken to be a neutral term, something that simply describes a relationship between means and ends, and so has argued that the School Effectiveness Movement has facilitated the spurious belief that there was nothing problematic in their declarations. This, he says, has enticed researchers to think of the study of the effective school as a matter of mere empirical investigation: '...if there are no values involved, or if it is so evidently good, then all we need to do is get on and investigate it' (Bottery, 2000:115).

Similarly, Blake *et al* (1998:132) have argued: 'It is the notion of effectiveness, and its close relation efficiency, that have above all replaced proper consideration of ends'. Pring (2005:13) has likewise proposed that the effectiveness debate has severed educational from moral discourses resulting in 'a theory of effectiveness which ignores the question 'Effective for what?''. Again, Wrigley has argued that research surrounding school effectiveness 'avoids a debate about the *purposes* of education' and, moreover, 'sows the illusion that poverty can be overcome by schools alone, without a wider political struggle' (Wrigley, 2006:35 our emphasis). He attributes the same sort of effect to the School Improvement Movement which is 'virtually silent about the purpose of schooling' or where different 'styles of leadership ... are leading to' (Wrigley, 2006:38).

Managerialism is part of a culture where the devising of means has become a dominant activity and where 'consideration of values, of the ends to which means lead, no longer takes place to any significant extent...' (Blake *et al*, 1998:133; see also MacIntyre, 2007:74). In short, many observers are unified in their judgement that the term effective has been used instrumentally as a means for excluding issues that might call into doubt the neutrality or self-evident goodness of desired changes in public policy, in this case as they relate to management structures.

Since 2004, those who wish to become senior managers in state schools in England must hold, or be working towards, National Professional Qualifications for Headship (NPQH) for which they will be assessed against government determined specifications. These are called Standards: 'The Standards recognise the key role that headteachers play in engaging in the development and delivery of government policy and in raising and maintaining levels of attainment in schools in order to meet the needs of every child' (DfES, 2004). But the word standard carries multiple inflections. These range from bog standard, to something like the norm (as in a standard rail ticket), to British Standard (that implies dependable, high-class manufacturing), but also extends to meanings inferred by terms like raising the standard (DES, 1991), that evoke the rallying of a nation under an emblem and of binding it to a common cause, however mysterious or dubious. Thus standard as a general category does not represent clear purposes. The *National Standards for Headteachers* (DfES, 2004) lists the qualities, activities and attributes necessary for the job. These descriptors of the standards include maintaining effective partnerships, shaping the future, creating a productive learning community, ensuring that the school moves forward, carrying the vision forward, the pursuit of excellence, developing and maintaining effective strategies, and so on.

What is missing is acknowledgement of the normative or substantive domain that would give meaning to implied purposes. For example, there is no explicit discussion of what the content of an effective partnership might be. There are some 38 references to 'effective' in the eleven page document (effective: partnerships, teachers, life-long learning, assessment, corrective action, relationships, communication, team work, feedback, learning communities, strategies for staff action, planning, organising and collaboration) without any definition of the term. Similarly, there is no discussion about the values underlying 'visions' that various Headteachers might have, and how these might be disparate and problematic and how these differences might be addressed. Nor is there any consideration of whether all would agree that a school 'moving forward' should go in one direction rather than another.

In avoiding these underlying purposes the *National Standards for Headteachers* employ a technical language that contains values that are indefinite or sustain an instrumental discourse that dodges issues of a substantive nature. These issues remain implicit and unstated. Together with NPM it gives the appearance of providing technical solutions to educational problems and for some is clearly ideological: 'New managerialism ... is very clearly an ideological rather than simply a technical reform of higher education and one that is firmly based on interests concerning relations of power and dominance' (Deem and Brehony, 2005:231-2). For others it is a procedure for 'keeping silent about human values' and for strengthening neo-liberal ideology, while reinforcing 'the sense of inevitability and fatalism that neo-liberal politicians use to quell dissent' (Wrigley, 2006:38).

Trusting managerialism is therefore problematic because of its attachment to instrumental reason. Here reason is turned from an epistemological tool with contradicting, negating and disproving qualities to a procedure that services relations of power and dominance or is used to quell dissent – from a search for purpose and value to a consideration of means. For Horkheimer, who coined the term, instrumental reasoning involves 'the adequacy of procedures for purposes more or less taken for granted and supposedly self-explanatory. It attaches little importance to the question whether the purposes as such are reasonable' (Horkheimer, 2004:3): 'Reason is considered to come into its own when it ... accepts itself simply as a tool' (Horkheimer, 1974:vii-viii).

For Habermas, instrumental reason 'extends to the correct choice among strategies, the appropriate application of technologies and the efficient establishment of systems (with *presupposed* aims in *given* situations), it removes the total social framework of interests in which strategies are chosen, technologies applied, and systems established, from the scope of reflection and rational construction' (Habermas, 1971:82). In short, in its instrumental form critical rationality operates on the surface, on the development of techniques for solutions to preordained problems. Instrumentalism may discover efficient ways of thieving, as in Fagan teaching Oliver the skills of effective pick-pocketing (Dickens, 2007), but is unwilling or incapable of reflecting upon the issue of theft *per se*.

Beneath the apparent neutrality of managerialism are thus a set of assumptions and a body of knowledge that is unavailable for scrutiny. Because instrumental reasoning shuts down areas for interrogation, trust in it is not a neutral act and is 'not so agnostic about ends as it pretends' (Blake *et al*, 1998:132). While instrumentalism may attempt to assume an 'inert' quality, as in Hume and Schopenhauer (Hume,

1973:458; Schopenhauer, 1974:171), or masquerade as 'purely formal' as in Weber (1968:85-6), beneath this veneer are assumptions about the way life should or has to be.

For some, the avoidance of the substantive domain is sufficient to unravel the fallacy that reason can serve as an inert or formal tool. Marcuse (1972) has suggested that 'formal' rationality in Weber actually coincides with 'capitalist rationality' (Marcuse, 1972:205-6). Trust in instrumental reasoning is therefore trust in an unstated normative agenda, a political *a priori* or an unclaimed purpose that imports substantive values under the guise of ethical neutrality.

The sequestered premises that underpin managerialism are arguably performativity and surveillance that, in capitalist economies, are secured by the effective management, monitoring and social adjustment of labour. If this were true for some it would help explain the depoliticisation of the public sphere as a site of potential instability as well as the associated fragmentation of communities and crises of political legitimation (Taylor, 1992; Habermas 1988). It would also help to explain how managerialism and the talk of effectiveness is 'inseparable from a mode of human existence in which the contrivance of means is in central part the manipulation of human beings into compliant patterns of behaviour' (MacIntyre, 2007:74).

Pupil voice

In 2008 the government published *Working Together: Listening to the voices of children and young people* (DCSF, 2008). The guidance aimed to help schools implement their legal requirement that pupils be consulted 'in connection with the taking of decisions which affect them' (*ibid*:2). The drivers underpinning the initiative were said to be children's rights, active citizenship, school improvement and personalisation (DCSF, 2007), and, under Section 7 of the 2005 Education Act, schools would be inspected by Ofsted for their provision. The document said that the reason for the policy was that children and young adults could 'contribute to the school's improvement' and that this would help nurture them to become 'confident individuals and responsible citizens' (*ibid*:3). Giving pupils a voice and involving them in school decision making processes was said to ensure they felt 'trusted and valued' (*ibid*:8).

But running alongside this narrative was another that would have the effect of restricting pupil voice and the degree of trust. Sometimes this was intimated in the way schools should merely 'take account' of pupils' views, or by the suggestion that pupils could 'contribute' to school policy, rather than co-construct it. But the restriction was also intimated in what was not said. For example, while reference was made to various 'levels of participation' there was no indication whether schools were being encouraged to move swiftly to the ultimate level where 'children share power and responsibility for decision-making'. Moreover, while it suggested that pupil voice could 'enhance curriculum provision' (*ibid*:8), it remained unstated whether this might possibly involve negotiating changes in provision. In places, however, the restrictions were voiced quite explicitly. We read that schools should 'manage expectations, i.e. explaining what is 'out-of-bounds', for practical, legal or political reasons' (*ibid*:11) and that it was school management 'who has the final say' (*ibid*:13). On the one hand, then, pupil voice was said to be necessary for cultivating confidence and trust in rational negotiation, but on the other, institutional parameters were set that clearly limited the extent of what was permissible. This is indicative of an epistemological dilemma.

In the first section we set out to explain why liberal epistemologists like Mill valued the 'voice' of rationality. Gadamer, too, has argued that 'we can never escape from the obligation of seeking to validate claims to truth through argumentation and opening ourselves to the criticisms of others' (Gadamer, 1975; see Bernstein, 1983). Pupil voice in citizenship education has drawn heavily upon this philosophical tradition: ''Talk' or discourse is obviously fundamental to active citizenship' (QCA, 1998:par 3.4); 'open and informed debate is vital for a healthy democracy' (*ibid*:par 1.9). But the limitations of such philosophically abstract notions of discourse and debate are not addressed. Gadamer's (1975:261) claim that dialogue is 'an ontological structural element in understanding' underplays the significance of varying social and political contexts in which discourses operate. As a philosophical notion it distances itself from issues concerning the *intentions* of those in dialogue, minimises the significance of the social or political *power* of contenders and refuses to question why participants might choose, or choose not, to validate the practical consequences of engagement. In essence, the limitation of liberal epistemology is that it provides merely a philosophical model of rational encounter that finds its own way into social and political practice.

Various political theories have filled the vacuum. Marx had argued that the case liberals made for the free exchange of ideas was inexorably tied to the economic world, to the free exchange of commodities, so that with the expansion of industrial capitalism the reality of free exchange in either domain, be it economic or ideational, became patently illusory for the majority. Liberalism, he claimed, gave one merely an 'abstract model of existence of free individuality' (Marx, 1973). The implication is that liberal philosophers like Mill and Gadamer leave dialogue at the level of abstraction and forsake the social and political fabric that enables or distorts genuine encounter. In stressing that dialogue is underpinned by notions of mutuality and respect, that it can result in genuine novelty in understanding and that it demands openness to risk and to the testing of one's opinions, there is presumed a community of un-alienated, un-cynical and committed participants. It is why Habermas has taken liberal epistemology, critiqued its assumptions and wedded to it the need for a transformative critique of social contexts that would impede dialogue:

> The ontological illusion of pure theory behind which knowledge-constitutive interests become invisible promotes the fiction that Socratic dialogue is possible everywhere and at any time... It is pure theory, wanting to derive everything from itself, that succumbs to unacknowledged external conditions and becomes ideological. (Habermas, 1972:314)

Pupil voice too suffers from this 'ontological illusion'. In school contexts, the invisibility of knowledge-constitutive interests lies not in the conjuror's art where management-as-power-holder would attempt to trick pupils into believing that institutional power is absent, but by a sleight of hand in which they would try to make themselves look invisible. The illusion has a number of implications for rationality and trust in pupil voice.

First, there is a need to unravel and problematise abstract notions of debate and discussion both within and outside the classroom. Pupil voice in school council meetings or classroom debates currently acts as if it should mimic the procedures of discourses that go on outside, in Parliament, between political parties and the electorate, in town councils, and the like. Underlying it, however, is the omission of a theory of power that determines or distorts dialogue and that preferences instrumental terms like 'communication' implying it is a skill without content (see Gibson, 2009).

The inadequacy has two consequences. It means that the complexity of media discourses and their linkage with political agendas *beyond* the school gates – that affect school policies and practices including pupil voice within it – are not made fundamental to the curriculum or to pupils' understanding of how voice works. It also means that power structures that determine, restrict or enable discussion *within* a school are inadequately addressed. Take citizenship education that aims at establishing 'a classroom climate in which all pupils are free from any fear of expressing *reasonable points of view* which contradict those held either by their class teacher or by their peers' (QCA, 1998:par 10.9, our italics). The notion that teachers are responsible for judging what is 'reasonable' glosses complex and highly questionable areas that are not eased by the circular reference to their 'professional judgement'.

Second, unbounded dialogue bereft of 'topic control' (Fairclough, 2002) can end up in many places. Whitty and Wisby note that 'genuine provision for pupil voice requires some power and influence to be passed to pupils, at which point it becomes unpredictable' (Whitty and Wisby, 2007a:4). The unpredictability to which they refer is the epistemological uncertainly of where encounter may roam; a foible of unpoliced argument and untrammelled reflection. It presents a conundrum. If pupils have or can learn through engagement the skills, values and knowledge that would make encounter genuine, the ends are unpredictable for the outcomes cannot be known. But, if pupils are deemed insufficiently knowledgeable or rational, the edifice of pupil voice and the enactment of human rights through consultation collapses. There is, in short, a distinction between '*who* has the final say' and '*what* is the final say'.

One conclusion may be that pupils, commonly from 'advantaged backgrounds' (Whitty and Wisby, 2007b:314; Arnot and Reay, 2007), are predestined to hallmark the knowledge-constitutive interests contained in pupil voice by being hoodwinked into believing they are rational teleologists empowered to critique the panoply of customs, policies and decisions that affect their school daily. Either that or they connive with school management to render the process sound by engaging with critical rationality at a level that is, in Whitty and Wisby's terms, predicable (ie controllable).

Third, in the process, trust fairs badly. The amount of trust pupils have in schools would appear to diminish annually. The latest annual NFER survey (Benton *et al*, 2008) on citizenship education has emphasised that while 'the important fact to underline about the introduction of citizenship education is that one of its key aims is the development of young people's trust' (p30), it observes the opposite: 'declining levels of trust in authority figures and institutions, including family and teachers' (Benton *et al*, 2008:vii).

Some warn of pupil voice becoming 'an instrument of teacher or state purposes' (Fielding, 2004:306), of it being reduced to a management tool that services performativity and surveillance. Others say that 'the egalitarian mythology of voice as a concept provides a valuable legitimating tool for any government keen to shift attention away from increasingly aggravated social inequalities' (Arnot and Reay, 2007:311). Others argue that 'policy makers and schools should beware of viewing pupil voice as merely a means of supporting the current policy agenda', of '...the danger that pupil voice...could produce a cohort of young people who are cynical about democratic processes' (Whitty and Wisby, 2007a:4).

These are views that would at least help explain pupils' current lack of trust. Coady (1992:vii) has suggested that people have a *prima facie* right to trust what others say, that 'our trust in the word of others is fundamental to the very idea of serious cognitive activity'. But in terms of pupil voice it is a claim that invites suspicion. Our stance would be that trust cannot be universal but is relative to context or institution: '...in unfavourable climates, our default stance should be distrust... If climate, domain, consequences, and metastances of trust or distrust are the important variables determining how much evidence is warranted before trusting, we can see why there can be no answer as to the appropriate stance to take toward testimony in general' (Jones, 1999:71-2).

Finally, we note that despite a growing corpus of scepticism surrounding pupil voice as currently constituted in schools, many, like Fielding, Whitty and Wisby, and Arnot and Reay, hold on to the belief in dialogue underlying liberal epistemology and the transformative potential of rational reflection and genuine encounter in schools. Transference of power does happen in some schools where trust is arguably higher. One small but significant example is Summerhill, a private English school with its policies of voluntary attendance at lessons, equal voting rights for both students and staff at the weekly School Meeting and an enthusiasm for open debate before rules are made collectively, and which has quite different intentions and may provide a genuine alternative (see Anderson, 2002; Print *et al*, 2002).

Failing that, more conventional state schools in England run the risk of developing sophisticated ways of engineering debate and discussion that 'end up betraying... interests, accommodating them to the *status quo*, and in a whole variety of ways reinforcing assumptions and approaches that are destructive of anything that could be considered remotely empowering' (Fielding, 2001:124). How a pupil might judge their particular school context and learn to move between trust and critical rationality at various times and in various ways within the current climate is beyond our ken.

Conclusion

In this chapter we have explored some of the links between critical rationality and trust. In the section on managerialism we suggested that reasoning has been employed instrumentally and that this approach was flawed insofar as it deflected more complex issues associated with substantive rationality where what is trustworthy, in terms of values and purposes, is highly contestable. In the section on pupil voice we argued that, while both the government and many of its principal proponents extol the virtues of critical rationality and encounter in schools, in reality this has often been bound to predicable and controllable ends within a context where pupils' trust in school authority declines year on year.

Given space, we could have extended the encounter between rationality and trust to areas of the curriculum like religious education. We have referred to the dominant liberal paradigm since the Enlightenment as being one of reliance upon critical rationality and scepticism. However, today in many schools the truth claims made by pre-modern religions have had to be interpreted through this rationalist model. Some have argued that it is a process designed to emasculate such claims by subjecting them to a mode of enquiry designed to ensure they become either personal or untrustworthy (see Locke, 1812; Collier,

1994; Wright, 2004). What is evident is that rationality cannot maintain the pretence that it is inert. Knowing how critical rationality is deployed, as well as what epistemic assumptions underpin any particular use of it, has fundamental implications for what and when one should trust, in education and beyond.

References

Anderson, J (2002) Questions of democracy, territoriality and globalisation. In Anderson, J (ed) *Transnational Democracy: Political spaces and border crossings.* London: Routledge

Arnot, M and Reay, D (2007) A Sociology of Pedagogic Voice: Power, inequality and pupil consultation. *Discourse: studies in the cultural politics of education* 28(3) p311-325

Baier, A (1986) Trust and Antitrust. *Ethics.* 96 (2) p231-260

Baier, A (2004) Demoralization, Trust, and the Virtues. In Calhoun, C (ed). *Setting the Moral Compass: Essays by Women Philosophers.* New York: Oxford University Press

Ball, S (2008) *The Education Debate.* Bristol: Policy Press

Benton, T, Cleaver, W, Featherstone, G, Kerr, D, Lopes, J and Whitby, K (2008) *Citizenship Education Longitudinal Study (CELS): Sixth Annual Report.* London: NFER

Berita Calvary (2010) *An Obituary printed in the London Times.* http://beritacalvary.blogspot.com/2008/09/obituary-printed-in-london-times.html (accessed 15th May 2010)

Bernstein, RJ (1983) *Beyond Objectivism and Relativism: Science, hermeneutics, and praxis.* Oxford: Blackwell

Blake, N, Smeyers, P, Smith, R and Standish, P (1998) *Thinking Again: Education after postmodernism.* London: Bergin and Garvey

Bottery, M (2000) *Education, Policy and Ethics.* London: Continuum

Coady, CAJ (1992) *Testimony: A philosophical study.* Oxford: Clarendon Press

Collier, A (1994) *Critical Realism: An introduction to Roy Bhaskar's philosophy.* London: Verso

Daily Telegraph (2009) Climate change: this is the worst scientific scandal of our generation, http://www.telegraph.co.uk/comment/columnists/christopherbooker (accessed 28th November 2009)

DCSF (Department for Children, Schools and Families) (2008) *Working Together: Listening to the voices of children and young people.* London: DCSF

DCSF (Department for Children, Schools and Families) (2007) *Real Decision Making? School councils in action – DCSF-RB-001.* London

Deem, R and Brehony, K (2005) Management as ideology: the case of 'new managerialism' in higher education. *Oxford Review of Education* 31(2) p217-235

DES (Department for Education and Science) (1991) *Citizen's Charter: The parent's charter.* London: HMSO

Descartes, R (1962) *Philosophical Writings.* London: Nelson

DfES (Department for Education and Skills) (2004) *National Standards for Headteachers.* London: DfES

Dickens, C (2007) *Oliver Twist.* London: Penguin Classics

Fairclough, N (2002) *Language and Power (Second Edition).* London: Longman Pearson Educational

Fielding, M (2001) Students as radical agents of change. *Journal of Educational Change.* (2) p123-141

Fielding, M (2004) Transformative approaches to student voice: theoretical underpinnings, recalcitrant realities. *British Educational Research Journal* 30(2) p295-311

Fukuyama, F (1995) *Trust: Social virtues and the creation of prosperity*. New York: Free Press

Gadamer, HG (1975) *Truth and Method*. London: Sheed and Ward

Gibson, H (2009) The Teaching of Democracy: Challenging the meaning of participation, discourse and dissent in the English school curriculum. *Citizenship, Social and Economics Education: An International Journal*, 8(1) p5-18

Gramsci, A (1971) *Selections from the Prison Notebooks of Antonio Gramsci*. London: Lawrence and Wishart

Habermas, J (1971) *Toward a Rational Society: Student protest, science, and politics*. London: Heinemann

Habermas, J (1972) *Knowledge and Human Interests*. London: Heinemann

Habermas, J (1988) *Legitimation Crisis*. Cambridge: Polity Press

Hardwig, J (1991) The Role of Trust in Knowledge. *The Journal of Philosophy* 88(12) p693-708

Hegel, GWF (1952) *The Philosophy of History*. New York: Dover

Hegel, GWF (1977) *Phenomenology of Spirit*. Oxford: Oxford University Press

Horkheimer, M (1974) *Critique of Instrumental Reason*. New York: Continuum

Horkheimer, M (2004) *Eclipse of Reason*. New York: Continuum

Hume, D (1973) *A Treatise of Human Nature*. Oxford: Oxford University Press.

Jones, K (1999) Second-Hand Moral Knowledge. *Journal of Philosophy* 96(2) p55-78

Kuhn, TS (1970) *The Structure of Scientific Revolutions*. Chicago: University of Chicago Press

Locke, J (1812) *An Essay Concerning Human Understanding: Volume II*. London: Thomas Davison

MacIntyre, A (2007) *After Virtue: A study in moral theory (Third Edition)*. London: Duckworth

Marcuse, H (1972) *Negations: Essays in Critical Theory*. Harmondsworth: Penguin

Marx, K (1973) *Grundrisse: Introduction to the critique of political economy*. London: Pelican

McGuigan. J (2006) *Modernity and Postmodern Culture (Second Edition)*. Buckingham: Open University Press

McLeod, C (2006) *Self-Trust and Reproductive Autonomy*. Cambridge, MA: MIT Press

Mill, JS (1859) On liberty. In Warnock, M (ed) (1969) *Utilitarianism and On Liberty*. London: Fontana

Paine, T (1986) *Common Sense*. New York: Penguin Classic

Pring, R (2005) *Philosophy of Education: Aims, theory, common sense and research*. London: Continuum

Pring, R (2007) *Philosophy of Education Research (Second Edition)*. London: Continuum

Print, M, Ornstrom, S and Skovgaard, N (2002) Education for Democratic Processes in Schools and Classrooms. *European Journal of Education* 37(2) p193-210

Putnam, RD (1995) *Bowling Alone: The Collapse and Revival of American Community*. New York: Simon and Schuster

QCA (Qualifications and Curriculum Council) (1998) *Citizenship and the Teaching of Democracy in Schools: final report of the Advisory Group on Citizenship (Crick Report)*. London.

Reynolds, D and Cuttance, P (eds) (1992) *School Effectiveness: Research, policy and practice*. London: Cassell

Schopenhauer, A (1974) *On the Fourfold Root of the Principle of Sufficient Reason*. La Salle: Open Court

Taylor, C (1992) *The Ethics of Authenticity*. Cambridge, MA: Harvard University Press

Teddlie, C and Reynolds, D (2000) *The International Handbook of School Effectiveness Research*. London: Falmer Press

Teddlie, C and Stringfield, S (1993) *Schools Do Make a Difference: Lessons learned from a 10 year study of school effects*. New York: New York Teachers College Press

Tubbs, N (1997) *Contradiction of Enlightenment: Hegel and the broken middle*. Aldershot: Ashgate Publishing

Webb, MO (1993) Why I Know About as Much as You: A reply to Hardwig. *The Journal of Philosophy* 90(5) p260-270

Weber, M (1968) *Economy and Society*. New York: Bedminister Press

Whitty, G and Wisby, E (2007a) *Real Decision Making? School councils in action*. London: Department for Children, Schools and Families

Whitty, G and Wisby, E (2007b) 'Whose voice? An exploration of the current policy interest in pupils involvement in school decision-making'. *International Studies in Sociology of Education* 17(3) p303-319

Wilkinson, R and Pickett, K (2009) *The Spirit Level*. London: Allen Lane

Wrigley, T (2006) *Another school is possible*. London: Bookmarks and Trentham

Wright, A (2004) *Religion, Education and Post-modernity*. London: Routledge Falmer

8

On the edge of chaos: inner city schools and the unequal burden of uncertainty

EWA SIDORENKO

> Teachers may be reluctant to admit to problems which may reflect on their professional competence. Heads may be unwilling to admit to running a difficult school. There seems to be a conspiracy of silence among those concerned, based partly on the faith that if you don't talk about problems they will go away, or conversely that if you do, it will magnify them (Lawrence *et al*, 1984:3)

It has become difficult to talk about the phenomenon of disorder in UK schools. Too many concepts cover or just intimate this issue: poor discipline, bad behaviour, deviance, urban youth, disaffection, failing schools, minority ethnic underachievement, or that of black boys, and white working class boys. In this paper I focus on the phenomenon of disorder in the classroom, or the school itself, which is readily recognised as a serious but rare contemporary issue by teachers (Press Releases from NAUSTW, 2009-2010), and tirelessly tackled without much success by Government initiatives yet often silenced/denied by academic literature as a construct (Gamarnikov and Green, 1999; Archer *et al*, 2010). What I want to examine is disorder as symptomatic of systemic problems within education. Unlike others however, I am not going to pre-empt this examination by claiming that school disorder exists discursively as a contemporary form of moral panic. Instead, I am interested in looking at school disorder as dynamic, and in considering the complex web of agencies involved.

Inner city schools: sites of order or chaos?

I begin by referring to the excellent French film *The Class* (Cantet, 2008) which received much attention from both the film critics and educational communities. This docudrama, written jointly by the scriptwriter Francois Begaudeauand the school students themselves through workshops, illustrates the ever-present conflict lurking in the classroom of the adolescent, multicultural, Parisian school in a difficult neighbourhood. Conflict erupts across a limited number of division lines: teacher against student(s), the most common; student against student, often over issues touching on ethnicity.

Much of the time, the teacher faces low level resistance or disruption to the tasks he sets, and yet he is tirelessly determined to turn every negative or challenging comment made by his pupils into something pedagogically useful. In other words, the teacher continues to try hard to engage his difficult students in teaching them new words and concepts, stretching them and validating anything they offer. Yet, conflicts keep erupting; chaos is a recurring feature in the classroom. There is a scene in the staffroom where a Design Technology teacher loses self-control, has an angry outburst and then a minor breakdown following a difficult lesson. Other teachers are momentarily stunned but no one is genuinely surprised, let alone shocked. In the staffroom, the emotional stain is palpable, the stress is well understood but there is no solution.

When you talk privately to teachers you soon acquire an anecdotal catalogue of rather shocking incidents: an indecent exposure by a teenage boy during an English lesson given by a female teacher; a boy simulating copulation with a doorframe during a lesson witnessed by a female Religious Studies teacher; a boy standing on a desk and refusing to get down; a teacher being sworn at, and many more cases.

The problem with referring to these situations is that there is no ready shared language which we can use to communicate the phenomenon without some kind of detailed description (Geertz, 1973). Ethnography is a good way to outline the issue, so is a reputable film document. Snapshots are not enough, chaos needs description; it needs context. In other words, disorder needs thick dramatic descriptions in order to convey the complex dynamics of the social event.

The reason for this is as follows. Social order is, as we know from classical sociology, the product of either consensus (Durkheim, 1984), cultural effects of legitimate authority (Weber, 1968; Giddens, 1971), or effective dominance of one group over another (Marx and Engels, 1967; Giddens, 1971), or, as we know from more contemporary thought, a more diffused operation of power through the self (Foucault, 1977), or an ethnomethodological joint ongoing accomplishment by social members. Disorder, or the breakdown of order, is a different phenomenon, which defies the rules of language. Order thus seems relatively easy to name; although how order is accomplished has been indeed the stuff of the entire sociological legacy. By contrast, disorder cannot easily be named. To say that a student, or a group of students, is disruptive does not in itself either give enough information about the nature of the problem, neither does it signal a solution to the problem. Disorder is accompanied by a release of emotional charge with the simultaneous shrinking of the human faculty of self-control; in effect, the breakdown, albeit temporary, of common rules and bonds. In other words, disorder is incoherent; it cannot be easily articulated.

What seems clear then, is that where conflict and chaos occur, the process of naming, and indeed describing, the phenomenon needs to address issues of dynamics, temporality, and, importantly, agency. Hence, many existing references to disorder in schools which talk of failing schools, disaffected youth or disruptive behaviour of failing boys (or any group) do not capture the complexity of the dynamics involved. Most of those references reduce the complexity to just one aspect: eg the concept of failing schools suggests that the problem lies with the school organisation; the idea of behaviour problems leads discussions to the issues of special needs, and there are ample popular common sense ideas about the causality of uncooperative parents. The latter, the notion of culturally deficient communities, whilst most problematic for the academic community, reduce the issue to the dysfunctional presentation of the difficult student to the detriment of other corresponding dynamic factors.

The issue of school chaos or, if we prefer, frequently recurring classroom disorder, problematises existing epistemologies of the issue. Because, as I said earlier, disorder is incoherent and cannot easily be articulated, existing sociological tools, which since Durkheim and Marx have been developed to theorise social order, are inadequate.

What we need is a recognition of anomic processes (Durkheim, 1984, 2002). Durkheim has given us a useful concept to name the condition of the breakdown of rules but we need to go further. We need to focus on those processes of disorder. Thus, an element of understanding of what actually happens is gained by looking at the agency involved. Psychology provides us with valuable insights into understanding individual pathology. Sociology, on the other hand, provides us with an understanding of the context in which agencies are placed. So what seems to be useful here is an approach which is able to examine the dynamics between all the elements: structure (cultural and material) and agency (cultural and material, including psychological) interacting in time and space. The issue of temporality, and thus fluidity, is very important because, despite asserting social change as a permanent feature of human history, sociology has tended to talk of reality in synchronic terms (de Saussure, 1983). What we need is a diachronically sensitive epistemology that, in its description and analysis, can account for a range of states so to speak, occurring within a short time: order followed by disorder, followed by order again. And so on.

Complexity theory provides us with concepts to do just that. Open systems, such as the school or the classroom, cannot be described as having stable order because they interact with their environment. Consequently, order, or to use the technical term, equilibrium, is always temporary, because, '[t]here has to be a constant flow of energy to maintain the organisation of the system' (Smith and Jenks, 2006:13). Rather than consider the contemporary school setting as one characterised *a priori* by equilibrium or order, complexity theory reveals that we need to treat open systems, such as the classroom, as far-from-equilibrium (Prigogine, 1996).

As the character of all the elements of the system within the classroom – the teacher, students, the organisation of work, curricular demands, testing regime and individual situations at hand – frequently change, and interact constantly, the energy needed to sustain the system will vary. This means that at times order will break down, and, after a time of disorder it will be restored.

To sum up: the examination of the problematic of school conflict/chaos needs an approach which is sensitive both to its institutional setting and to the dynamics of agencies involved not as isolated, separate phenomena but rather, as elements of a complex, dynamic, far-from-equilibrium system. This approach promises to identify insights into those elements of the systems which need re-thinking and perhaps, lend themselves to re-forming.

Structure or agency?

Before moving on to a specific example in order to analyse some of those dynamic elements, let us rehearse in a little more detail what has already been said, through separate analyses about the issue of school disorder.

Generally, there are two broad approaches here: first, the structural explanation, and second, the agency explanation. The structural explanation has emerged within the sociology of education primarily as Marxist or late Marxist tradition, with emphasis placed on the hidden structures of power which work against the needs of the subjugated social groups, but instead, reproduce social division in order to serve the needs of capitalist economy. These structural explanations, however, quite early on within the sociology of education turned to analysing the operations of culture. Yet, the cultural explanations (Gramsci, 1991; Bourdieu and Passeron, 1977; Bernstein, 1973) continued to remain within the structural paradigm, ie, regard culture as structurally determinant. Thus, despite turning to softer type of causality, they remained to perceive unequal educational outcomes as structurally necessary for capitalism. Interestingly, this perspective continued to ignore the agency factor despite identifying the clear agency articulations of resistance to schooling (Willis, 1977).

In the more contemporary debates, structural explanations of critical sociology of education have tended to problematise common sense and policy articulations of discourses of cultural deficit (Gamarnikov and Green, 1999). The discourse of cultural deficit attributed to a mixed bag of sources (ranging from a specific reading of Bourdieu and Bernstein, the Third Way ideas and New Labour policies, to popular tabloid media, and last, but not least, teachers' staffrooms) has been consistently challenged as pathologising the vulnerable communities.

In the most recent articulation of this, Archer *et al* (2010) observe that:

> [i]t is the latest development in an ongoing history of the pathologisation of urban spaces, in which they are constructed by the dominant imagination as 'rubbish' and 'shit', as dumping grounds that

> contain the socially excluded, 'unfit' and undesirable [...that] these labels transfer from urban spaces to urban schools and infect the identity work of their young students (Archer *et al*, 2010:2)

What we have here is a clear critique of the common sense pathologisation of urban spaces because of the damage that such labelling causes. The damage here consists in imposing negative images on local urban areas and, specifically, their young inhabitants, which then, through adolescents' identity work, infect their emerging identity and, presumably, what is not said in this quote: might cause them to oppose or reject educational opportunities. In other words, Archer *et al* (2010) move the discussion closer to recognising the importance of the outcome of 'identity work', ie of the character of agency thus forming, but the reductive suggestion that the urban spaces are subject to pathologisation from outside, as it were, remains.

What this model then does not encompass is the way in which agency feeds back into the system, and the way in which the system (of urban spaces) generates 'pathology' in return. Clearly, this idea is ethically and politically uncomfortable; the suggestion that 'damaged', vulnerable agency is not just a product of social structure, but that it also generates further pathology back into the system is hugely uncomfortable when what we are thinking about is young people. But in other disciplines we already analyse this dynamic, for instance when talking about cycles of child abuse.

Agency explanations accounting for disorder are a neglected part of mainstream sociology. Despite a clear indication of the active role of boys who reject educational opportunities (Willis, 1977) in favour of working class jobs in manufacturing in the 1970s and early 1980s, there has been little attention given to the agency of rejection as constituent of the school system itself. This way of thinking permeates the common sense accounts, which, it needs to be added, underplay the role of structure.

An interesting development in terms of theory has emerged from the new sociology of childhood, particularly from Corsaro (1997), who identified the culturally productive elements in the way in which children interpret culture around themselves. Rather than seeing children as vessels of cultural transmission, unreflexively reproducing culture, Corsaro (1997) shows, with his ethnographic work, that children are engaged in interpretive reproduction of adult rules. Reproduction therefore is not perfect; it is subject to collective interpretations. Here we have an epistemological shift away from the sociologically shaped tradition of seeing childhood in terms of socialisation; a modern version of Locke's *tabula rasa*. That nurture-sensitive developmental psychology has already established agency as present from birth through the entire process of development is no longer new. Yet, despite this, sociology, particularly that dominated by the constructivist (or post-structuralist) ideas continues to ignore the issue of agency in examining school conflict or disorder.

What we need, then, to be able to understand how schools fail to arrive at the outcomes they set out, is to look at them through a complexity theory perspective. The concept of social ecology enables a description of pupils, the classroom and the school, as a set of interrelated systems. Just like natural ecology, social ecology is characterised by certain properties.

First, the constituent systems are interrelated. Bad teaching will result in poor learning (not for all learners, but for some). Equally, challenging behaviour of learners might result in a cycle of negativity in the classroom, to a greater or lesser extent. And so on.

Clearly then, social order within the classroom is an emergent property (and the closest sociology has come to articulate this point was from the tradition of ethnomethodology). In natural systems, this means that order needs a stable supply of energy. It is difficult to talk about energy in relation to human interaction, yet we know from the sociological tradition that this energy could be thought about in terms of consensus (Durkheim) or domination (Marx) or authority (Weber, and, arguably, Foucault etc).

The point is that for order to emerge in the classroom, it is not just the institutional and material setting (structure) that needs to be provided, the learner, through their agency, also needs to provide or feed some input into the system, so that order can emerge, and learning can take place. In other words, the learner needs to be willing to accept the rules of the game.

We are now finding from psychology that for some young people it is very difficult to supply a stable flow of trust, in its socio-psychological function, and participation in the school setting, and hence the learning processes. That then means that the classroom ecology is composed of agency (or agencies) which could be characterised by the unstable supply of trust. More formally, we could say that elements of such a social ecology are ontologically unstable, and hence make this a volatile system.

Naturally, it is hugely important that we enquire about the reasons why so many young people are unable to provide a consistent attitude or behaviour in those settings. Equally, we need to ask whether the current institutional arrangements are indeed capable of embracing and effectively delivering the environment necessary to generate trust in vulnerable learners. So, to take the complexity perspective is not just to inject uncomfortable questions from psychology into sociology (for instance: 'what's wrong with the learners?') but also, through a psychological insight we can interrogate the institutional framework and ask: 'what's wrong with the school and the educational system itself'? These are perfectly legitimate questions providing they are dealt with in a complex, rather than reductive way.

Thick description of chaos

To be able to grasp the character of cases of chaos in schools one would have to spend time in them. A teacher said to me: 'you cannot explain this to anyone outside. You would have to be there'. Whilst we do know about gangs, inner city problems, deprived communities etc, we don't really have much awareness of the character and the scale of disruption which happens within the walls of inner city schools. Jean Lawrence, a retired former principal lecturer in education at Goldsmiths College, writing in 2006 about her experience as a head of a south London comprehensive school in the late 1960s, said,

> No one but me and my brilliant deputy Margaret Tucker, of blessed memory, knew the full situation. Margaret and I picked up faeces from toilet floors, and dragged soiled sanitary towels from behind radiators, while our juvenile schizophrenic on all fours butted her head against swinging classroom doors, and hallucinated that bats were flying in through closed windows. A sick head of department flicked paper pellets with a ruler from a second floor window into the playground, one teacher pinioned a girl against the wall in a frenzy of anger, while another shouted at the recently arrived Caribbean children to go back where they belonged. (Lawrence, 2006)

Shocking as this may be, such snapshots of chaos, as argued earlier, do not convey the full context.

A good way of documenting the social ecology of the classroom is through ethnography. In her study of a white working class community in Bermondsey, southeast London, Evans (2006) explores how primary school boys from working class families navigate their lives around schooling, street and home life. She accounts for disruptive behaviour by these boys in school by analysing the dynamic interplay between the school set-up and children's agencies. It is worth citing here the specific elements of this dynamic: thirty 10-11 year old children, the teacher, teaching assistant, existing peer groups with their internal ranking and alliances, influence from street culture to which disruptive boys tend to belong, influence from parents, and formal school expectations of a specific type of embodied behaviour. By the latter, Evans means a degree of bodily self-control needed for a sustained period of concentrated work whilst sitting down at a table, largely absent from the cultural capital of the disruptive boys.

Evans compares frequent eruptions of chaos in Tetner Ground Primary School to *Lord of the Flies*, only without the desert island, and plenty of adults are looking on in vain, as, everywhere, danger looms (Evans, 2006:116). She argues that, although there may be underlying special needs which exacerbate the situation 'the problem of disruptive boys is a social one, to do with peer group formation in a school where adult authority is weak' (Evans, 2006:114). After school the boys tend to spend much of their time playing outside, without adult supervision or protection. There, in the streets, it is important for the boys to be allied to a group of peers or friendly older youths able to extend protection. The streets are not safe for the boys and so survival strategies are important. Being able to deploy threatening, aggressive behaviour is, according to Evans (2006:115), a form of 'social good'. The ability developed in the street is also useful and valued within the school where it becomes a form of prestige seeking. There is, then, a clear link between street culture and the peer group dynamics within the school. At times, conforming to school expectations of engaging in a particular task might clash with the needs of the peer group demands; boys who refuse to fulfil the calls of their peer group risk losing protection both within and outside the school (Evans, 2006).

What is also fascinating in this study is that Evans, who followed the boys' lives quite closely, testified that some of the most disruptive boys were very different at home. They were not lacking attention or love; they behaved in normal and quite affectionate ways with their mothers. Their disruptive identity belonged outside the home. Hence, Evans' conclusion is that it is in the formation of the disruptive boys' peer groups treated as a social phenomenon (Evans, 2006:83) that we need to look towards for answers about the issue of chaos in schools. To follow on from Evans' conclusion, I now turn to psychological dimensions involved in learning in order to see how peer groups and individual agency interact with the school setting.

Psychological dynamics: barriers to learning

So far in this chapter I have argued that in order to account for disorder in schools we need to draw on complexity theory to provide an examination of dynamic interactions which include social structural and agency factors. The context-bound character of chaos means that its analysis needs to begin with an ethnographic thick description. An ethnographic approach enables a coherent sketch of chaos to emerge, and so a closer examination of dynamic processes within the social ecology of the school in moments of crisis becomes possible.

In this section I turn to Illeris (2007) for a psychological explanation of barriers to learning in order to understand the pressures on, and from, agencies involved.

In the chapter 'Barriers to learning', Illeris (2007) lists three types of obstacles when learning is intended: mislearning, defence and resistance. Mislearning is the least problematic form; it is a problem of error, of content. This kind of problem can be easily rectified because agency is willing to learn.

Defence is an unconscious mental mechanism developed as a result of prior threatening experiences, which is activated (unconsciously) in similar situations. In the context of learning, defence protects individuals' mental balance, for instance, in the conditions of risk society when we are overwhelmed by negative information about global warming, the defence mechanism might lead to a denial of the problem. Illeris (2007) argues that we need such mechanisms in order to protect our mental health. Defence in a stronger version is also activated to protect identity. Identity defence helps agency to survive conditions which are perceived to be depriving them of control over their own lives. Defence then results in not learning, when learning is intended. Overcoming defence is possible only when agency has a 'strong core identity' (Illeris, 2007:161), or 'ontological security' (Giddens, 1991: 35) which will be explained later.

Finally, resistance is actively deployed by agency in the face of what is perceived to be unreasonable demands or circumstances (Illeris, 2007). These conditions can be seen by agency in 'cognitive terms [as] incomprehensible and unreasonable' (Illeris, 2007:170), and in affective terms are accompanied by levels of frustration. These conditions present as 'insurmountable obstacles that limit [...] life fulfilment' (Illeris, 2007:170). In children and young people this can present as difficult behaviour.

Let us consider the significance of the above characterisation of barriers to learning for the school setting. Clearly, the first barrier is not significant; its character is accidental and not systemic (unless the teacher who is in charge has inadequate subject knowledge and is teaching erroneous material). The two other barriers touch on more significant and difficult issues of a cultural and psychological nature when learners are overwhelmed or threatened by information, challenges, or the learning situation itself. This does present a systemic issue in the sense that there is no fit between the teaching objective and the learning capacity. In a significant way, the practice of differentiation aims to overcome just these kinds of issues. But it may well be that more needs to be addressed. Illeris (2007) argues that resistance, ie the active expression of rejection of the unacceptable learning situation, needs to be allowed in the school. Whilst resistance is often viewed by schools as something negative and disruptive, Illeris argues that

> it is often in connection to resistance, that the most important transcendent learning occurs. Personal development in particular, which is currently accorded such significance in education, often occurs through a process characterised by resistance. (Illeris, 2007:172)

It can also be argued that an expression of resistance or recognition of defence deployed by learners constitutes, what is considered by complexity theory, feedback which is crucially needed for systems to be able to adjust. In other words, if we really want learning to take place (as opposed to just keeping groups of adolescents off the streets), we need to understand learners' psychological challenges.

Identity work and schooling

According to Illeris (2007), learning needs to be looked at holistically; not just in terms of competence development but in the way in which the whole person of the learner interacts and changes through the process of learning: 'identity development can be understood as the individually specific essence of total learning' (Illeris, 2007:138). To do this, Illeris discusses a number of approaches, and as a starting point draws on Erikson's concept of identity development as one which includes both social and individual aspects and, significantly, one which evolves incrementally throughout the entire lifespan. However, Illeris departs from Erikson's conception of the adult personality as the conditions of late modernity have moved on from those described by Erikson in the late 1960s.

Illeris does not go as far as some of the postmodern identity theorists who see contemporary identity as totally fragmented, dissolved or empty of any core; this kind of state in reality would result in total incapacity, mental breakdown and, importantly, learning would not be possible had that been the case. Instead, Illeris agrees with Stern's concept of the core self (Stern, 1995 in Illeris, 2007), and with Giddens' ontological security (Giddens, 1991 in Illeris, 2007) as necessary for the learning process to be possible. However, in agreement with much postmodern work on identity, Illeris adds that the current societal conditions have moved the goal of identity development from stable to flexible.

So rather than aiming towards a 'more or less fixed identity as the goal of the process' (Illeris, 2007:139) under the conditions of modernity, today's society needs 'both a core identity and extreme flexibility, which must not have the nature of identity confusion but, rather, that of constant reconstruction' (Illeris, 2007:142). To develop this point in more detail Illeris turns to the work of another contemporary learning researcher, Kegan, who developed a detailed characterisation of complex lifelong transformations of orders of consciousness or personal development. Of the five transformative steps, the last three correspond to the general characterisation of Western societal development ie, step 3: the socialised mind, reachable by around age 6, is called traditionalism; step 4: the self-authoring mind, reachable in adolescent years, is called modernism, and step 5: the self-transforming mind is referred to as post-modernism. It is worth citing here the characterisation of the identity transformation in the final, fifth step:

> The possibility presents itself of exceeding the systems, liberating oneself from fixed ideologies, institutions and identities and achieving a general, dialectical order of consciousness where, on the basis of one's interpretation of the environment, one can make decisions about formulations, paradoxes, contradictions and relationships with other people and oneself. (Illeris, 2007:148 after Kegan, 1994)

And yet, as Illeris notices, many people may struggle to reach step 4 in which

> one can oneself control the more abstract matters such as generalisations, values, relations with others, role consciousness and self-awareness, and in this [step] one is controlled by abstract systems such as ideologies, institutions and identity. (Illeris, 2007:148 after Kegan, 1994)

We can see here that structural societal level demands become more and more challenging from the point of view of identity development. Illeris (2007) notices, for instance, that step 3 would have been the highest in Western Europe prior to the Enlightenment and the emergence of capitalism. Clearly, then, identity work becomes more and more challenging for the individual. Let us consider some implications from that.

First, it becomes clear, if we take this approach, that the widely commented-on fact of the fuzzy boundary separating adolescence and adulthood today and the prolonging of childhood, are not a problem but a normal outcome of the shifting of the goal-post of adulthood accomplishment. Had the goal remained at the level of acquiring of competence in terms of abstract systems (cognitively) and self-authorship (in identity), adulthood could indeed continue to be reachable in late teens. But after that stage there is one more to go through, one which moves individuals beyond abstract systems, into dialectical type cognition, and identity continues to evolve in processes of self-transformation.

Second, what Illeris mentions in passing, that most people today struggle to reach the penultimate step, appears significant in the context of discussion of identity work in schooling. We have seen from Evans' ethnography how significant, even for young pre-teen disruptive boys, is their position within their peer groups. In the context of schooling, and expectations of lifelong learning society, it is highly relevant to ask about the barriers to reaching the (presently) final step of identity transformation. Kegan shows us the degree of complexity of identity development needed in psychological terms. What we can conclude from this is that the development of the 'self-transforming mind' in the final transformative step is synonymous with successful educational experience in contemporary terms.

The issue, it could be argued, takes us at this point back into the realm of sociological enquiry; that is of social stratification. We already know much about educational class inequalities, particularly in the UK. As argued before in this paper, sociology has already touched on the convergence between educational outcomes and cultural difference of the learning agency. We may need, perhaps, to enquire about psychological processes involved in identity development of those young people who struggle in contemporary school settings; who do not provide the degree of motivation (agency input mentioned earlier) needed for them to engage in learning. In other words, we may have to develop psychologically sensitive class analysis of the identity development, as identity work is part of the process of learning.

Clearly, this proposition takes risks, as once again it can be criticised for leading to more pathologisation of the vulnerable sections of the community. Yet, let us not forget that, from the viewpoint of the complexity framework, the issue cannot be reduced to one aspect of the dynamic; it will also involve the examination of the system, ie the institutional context in which learners find themselves. This framework therefore does not need to blame the community and the student for not supplying the right learning identity (or agency); rather this approach will be able to comment on the approach that these students need, given their developmental characteristics. Given our society's recognition of the reality of change, and need for flexibility, why would we not want to question the appropriateness of the institutional setting developed, after all, under the societal conditions of deference in Victorian times? What makes us think that we can ever be successful trying to educate inner city youth growing up in socially deprived areas in institutions holding 1500 young people under one roof, when our culture by default celebrates individualism over any other idea?

Third, let us consider what the fifth stage of identity transformation actually might mean in terms of developing personal goals in contemporary society in class terms in the UK. From many writers we learn that contemporary goals (of adulthood) are flexibility and the ability to re-shape and re-construct our lives when the situation demands (Bauman, 2000; Giddens, 1991; Illeris, 2007). The goal of flexibility, as we know from Giddens and Illeris, is only possible with a strong core identity. So in order to be in a position to open oneself to the 'layers of extreme flexibility' (Illeris, 2007:142), first a solid core needs to be in place.

But how do young people develop the solid core under the material and cultural conditions of uncertainty? There, it seems to me, lies the class difference in terms of the possibility of developing such a solid base (and according to Kegan, we need to go through all stages, as each stage builds on the previous one). Children and young people living in families which are described as stable in terms of employment, mental health, material conditions, and ideally, but perhaps not crucially, good educational parental background can reach the fourth step (modernism) through the influence of modelling behaviour taken from the parents. Whether they go far in education and whether they will develop the flexibility needed for the changing economic conditions in future may depend on contingency; the point is, they have a chance to reach the learning and identity developmental stage necessary for the final, fifth stage.

On the other hand, when the starting point is a family or the immediate community which cannot offer a sense of stability (be it employment, economic, or in terms of mental health etc) it may be harder for young people to reach the level of self-regulation, self-formation, autonomy, individuation as constituent of self-authorship in modern identities. Moreover, if we read this process back to Erickson's stages of identity development, any unresolved crises from previous stages inhibit a successful resolution of the next. Thus it may well be possible that pre-school experiences may already result in difficulties in terms of behaviour expectations needed at even the primary level.

One example may be the disruptive boys' difficulties in holding themselves with the stillness required for literacy tasks by the school's expectations of 'embodied behaviour'. This ability, Evans (2006) argues, is considered ordinary at a very young age of just over 4, so 'Children who resist are considered to be abnormal yet it seems it is those who enjoy formal education early who are the 'more exceptional phenomenon" (Evans, 2006:cc).

Yet, it is not just the scholastic readiness that is an issue, as learning needs to be looked at holistically (Illeris, 2007). According to Erikson (1968) a poor (inadequate, inconsistent or harsh) quality of care received in the first year of life may well result in a low level of trust in the world, and in others which can negatively affect relationships with people, and hence, in everyday language, behaviour problems.

At this point it is worth reflecting on the institutional setting for children's identity development in primary schools. As Alexander (2010) noted, there is a strong contradiction between contemporary, post-Plowden English schooling at primary level where provision tends to be child-centred and, in the younger years, delivered in a less formalised way and the more prescriptive requirements of the Primary National Strategies (Alexander, 2010; Hofkins, 2003). The learning environment lacks visible elements of power, and teaching strategies encourage relaxed and collaborative work from children. Inevitably, such expectations will involve a degree of freedom (of movement, of being allowed to speak, to initiate ideas and action) as well as self-discipline given to and expected from children.

Anecdotally, from teachers we know that some of the most difficult behaviour in such an environment comes from children who have little freedom (or perhaps receive harsh discipline) at home. This obviously needs evidence from research but what is interesting, if that is the case, is that at least in some cases of difficult behaviour the relaxed school environment proves challenging (and perhaps confusing). This may well be because, paradoxically, the primary school in this country expects two accomplishments: early degree of self-control (in a relaxed environment) and early scholastic readiness (under the strict National Curriculum regime).

It appears then that these expectations in themselves can be very problematic for many children. This clearly points to the issue of class, but not so much in terms of the classical understanding of social class as a more contemporary marker, perhaps one more aligned with experiences of social exclusion which generate marked psychological differences in the level of readiness, or even identity development.

Thus, when the starting point for identity development in the context of educational setting is a socially disadvantaged background where stability of various kinds is not the basis for underpinning childhood experiences, the trajectory of development seems particularly uncertain. Not having role models in terms of qualifications or job identity; and thus not knowing (in the sense of seeing one's significant others engaged in successful life strategies which generate stability) what life choices are accessible presents a very difficult challenge for the adolescent identity work.

One could hypothesise that in Kegan's terms, young people from socially deprived backgrounds may well experience a trajectory which propels them from step 3 (traditionalism) towards step 5 (post-modernism) without having grounded their identity development in the more stable ideas of step 4 (modernism). In other words, from a degree of insecurity, these adolescents perceive the world of uncertainty which demands of them flexibility for which they are not ready. Perhaps it may be possible to deploy Illeris' barriers to learning analysis to identity development, and suggest that in the face of the uncertain world you can have young people adopting defence and resistance mechanisms against identity work itself, which is constituent of learning (Illeris, 2007).

By contrast, following on from the last point, let us briefly look at educationally most advantaged children whose background involves educationally and, or socially successful parents. In terms of the identity development as outlined above, these children find themselves in an interesting position in relation to contemporary life trajectory. Despite ultimately having to embrace the demands of flexibility and self-transformative attitudes (which could be characterised by uncertainty), there is no such uncertainty experienced by them in their formative years.

Socially advantaged parents tend to smooth the path of their children in terms of education so there actually is no uncertainty in their educational careers; not doing well in school is not an option (or conversely, a risk); expectations of a university degree as a norm shapes young children's ideas of the direction in which they are going. The direction towards good education is a decision which these children did not have to make themselves. So, in some ways, we could see that a privileged background is one in which elements of certainty, or in other words modernism, to use Kegan's category, are retained, and provide a secure basis from which to embrace the final step leading to the self-transforming mind.

Let us come back to the issue of identity work of adolescents in school settings and re-consider the school ecology from the point of view of the disadvantaged learner who is not doing well in school. In his holistic approach to learning, Illeris reminds us that identity work is what, developmentally, the period of adolescence is all about. In fact, constructing their identities is, for them, more urgent than the choice of career; 'in one way, it is also a precondition for their choice of career, or part of it' (Illeris, 2007:204).

> The school and education system developed primarily to deal with subject learning, while matters of identity in its broadest sense are what young people are concerned about. Therefore, young people react more or less reluctantly to the academic subject requirements, which for the most part are forced upon them, and which they often find outdated, while the representatives of the system attempt to keep the pupils' concentration on the academic work, which they themselves are trained in, are committed to, and are under an obligation to uphold. (Illeris, 2007:203)

If we now consider how these circumstances affect the experience of identity work for the disadvantaged students, the school is a site of multiple challenges and threats, from learning situations, when intended learning is resisted or when defence mechanisms are activated, when receiving negative feedback from teachers, when peer groups alliances demand engagement in ranking or prestige seeking behaviour. Pressures also come from other external sources and they may add to the overall difficulties in engagement in learning.

Conclusion

In this chapter I have argued that occurrences of chaos and disruptive behaviour can be treated as expressions of serious underlying systemic problems in contemporary school culture. Earlier in the chapter I argued after others that there seems to be unwillingness within the academic community to engage with this problem because of uncomfortable political implications. Yet, for two significant reasons this issue should be examined: first, because the level of stress in some schools is unacceptably high, and is one of the key reasons why so many teachers leave the profession (the stress is also the experience of children and young people in those schools, yet their voices are conspicuously absent from this picture). Second, because the difficult behaviour leading to serious disruption of learning and to breakdown of order is symptomatic of other significant problems.

On the one hand, there is the issue of supporting disadvantaged and socially excluded communities in the widest possible sense, but on the other hand, there is also the issue of reconsidering the design of compulsory schooling in such a way that it would actually be sensitive to the developmental (in the holistic sense) needs of its diverse student populations.

Following a close reading of Evans (2006) and Illeris (2007) I have also argued that the postmodern goal of flexible adulthood characterised by embracing life with uncertainty is unequally distributed in our society. Young people growing up in socially underprivileged communities may have uncertainty imposed on them by challenging life circumstances thus causing them to adopt identity defence mechanisms which render their educational experiences so much more difficult. It is also clear that some of the key elements within the school ecology are the dynamics of peer group development, as illustrated by Evans (2006). I have also concluded that, in those cases, the classroom ecology is at times composed of agencies characteristic of the unstable supply of trust.

This chapter, then, has argued that contemporary school culture does not recognise in its design the complex psychological challenges facing its diverse student populations. In conclusion, I would argue for a sensitive and thorough ethnographic methodology as a grounding for a new, psychologically informed sociological examination of class related school failure and disruptive behaviour within the framework of complexity theory which would consider dynamic relationships in the complex, emergent system that the school is.

References

Alexander, R (2010) (ed) *Children, Their World, Their Education. Final Report and Recommendations of the Cambridge Primary Review.* Cambridge: Routledge

Archer, L, Hollingworth, S, and Mendick, H (2010) *Urban Youth and Schooling.* Maidenhead: Open University Press

Bauman, Z (2000) *Liquid Modernity.* Cambridge: Polity Press

Bernstein, B (1973) *Class, Codes and Control: Vol 2.* London: Routledge and Kegan Paul

Bourdieu, P and Passeron, J (1977) *Reproduction in Education, Society and Culture.* London: Sage

Cantet, L (2008) *The Class*.
Corsaro, W (1997) *The Sociology of Childhood*. Thousand Oaks CA: Pine Forge Press
Durkheim, E (1984) *The Division of Labour in Society*. New York: The Free Press
Durkheim, E (2002) *Suicide*. London: Routledge
Erikson, E (1968) *Identity: youth and crisis*. New York: Norton
Evans, G (2006) *Educational Failure and Working Class White Children in Britain*. Basingstoke: Palgrave Macmillan
Foucault, M (1977) *Discipline and Punish: the birth of the prison*. New York: Vintage
Gamarnikow, E and Green, A (1999) The third way and social capital: education action zones and a new agenda for education, parents and community? *International Studies in Sociology of Education* 9(1) p3-22
Geertz, C (1973) *The Interpretation of Cultures*. New York: Basic Books
Giddens, A (1971) *Capitalism and Modern Social Theory: an analysis of the writings of Marx, Durkheim and Max Weber.* Cambridge: Cambridge University Press
Giddens, A (1991) *Modernity and Self Identity: self and society in the late modern age*. Stanford CA: Stanford University Press
Gramsci, A (1991) *Prison Notebooks*. New York: Columbia University Press
Hofkins, D (2003) National Primary Strategy. *TES Magazine*19 September 2003
Illeris, K (2007) *How We Learn: learning and non-learning in school and beyond*. London: Routledge
Lawrence, J (2006) Fifty years on, behaviour still holds us back. *TES Magazine* 27 January 2006
Lawrence, J, Steed, D and Young, P (1984) *Disruptive Children – Disruptive Schools*. Beckenham: Croom Helm
Marx, K and Engels, F (1967) *The Communist Manifesto*. New York: Penguin
Prigogine, I (1996) *The End of Certainty: time, chaos and the new laws of nature*. New York: The Free Press
de Saussure, F (1983) *Course in General Linguistics*. London: Duckworth
Smith, J and Jenks, C (2006) Qualitative Complexity: ecology, cognitive processes and the re-emergence of structure in the post-humanist social theory. London: Routledge
Weber, M, (1968) *Economy and Society*. New York: Bedminster Press
Willis, P (1977) *Learning to Labour*. New York: Columbia University Press

Recent Press releases from NASUWT:

Relief as Teacher Acquitted of Serious Charges. 29 April 2010 http://www.nasuwt.org.uk/Whatsnew/NASUWTNews/PressReleases/ReliefAsTeacherAquittedOfSeriousCharges/NASUWT_006390 (accessed 29 May 2010)
Stress and Lack of Support Leaving Some Teachers Suicidal. 5 April 2010 http://www.nasuwt.org.uk/Whatsnew/NASUWTNews/PressReleases/StressAndLackOfSupportLeavingSomeTeachersSuicidal/NASUWT_006294 (accessed 29 May 2010)
Employers Failing to Protect Teachers from Violence and Abuse. 5 April 2010 http://www.nasuwt.org.uk/Whatsnew/NASUWTNews/PressReleases/EmployersFailingToProtectTeachersFromViolenceAndAbuse/NASUWT_006271 (accessed 29 May 2010)
Criminality Violence and Bullying Blights Young Lives says the NASUWT. 19 March 2010 http://www.nasuwt.org.uk/Whatsnew/NASUWTNews/PressReleases/CriminalityViolenceAndBullyingBlightsYoungLivesSaysTheNASUWT/NASUWT_006115 (accessed 29 May 2010)
NASUWT Welcomes Tougher Criminal Penalties for those who Assault Teachers. 25 September 2009 http://www.nasuwt.org.uk/Whatsnew/NASUWTNews/PressReleases/NASUWTWelcomesTougherCriminalPenaltiesForThoseWhoAssaultTeachers/NASUWT_005144 (accessed 29 May 2010)

Contributors

Jo Backus is Senior Lecturer in Study of Religions and Philosophy and Ethics. She teaches modules focused on Judaism, Islam, Western and Eastern Philosophy (Buddhism), Citizenship and Religious Education. Her most recent publication was co-authored with Denise Cush on Buddhism within the English State School System.

Howard Gibson is Programme Leader for the full time Masters in Education at Bath Spa University, teaches modules on citizenship, discourse and power, and has recently published on issues connecting political philosophy with education, eg instrumental rationality (Oxford Review of Education), New Labour's parent policy (Canadian Journal of Educational Administration and Policy), the teaching of democracy (Citizenship, Social and Economics Education: An International Journal) and economics education (International Review of Economics Education). More importantly, he cycles everywhere.

David Gillborn is Professor of Critical Race Studies in Education at the Institute of Education, University of London. David has twice been recipient of the UK's most prestigious education research award, the Society for Educational Studies (SES) prize for outstanding education book of the year; for his books *Racism and Education: coincidence or conspiracy?* and *Rationing Education* (co-authored with Deborah Youdell). David has been honoured for his work 'promoting multicultural education' by the American Educational Research Association (AERA) special interest group on the *Critical Examination of Race, Ethnicity, Class and Gender in Education*. He is founding editor of *Race Ethnicity and Education*, the leading international journal on racism and education, and co-editor (with Ed Taylor and Gloria Ladson-Billings) of *Foundations of Critical Race Theory in Education*. In addition to his research and teaching, David works closely with policy and advocacy groups, including the Stephen Lawrence Charitable Trust, the Runnymede Trust and the National Children's Bureau.

Jill Jameson is Director of Research and Enterprise and Reader in Educational Research at the University of Greenwich. She specialises in educational leadership, e-learning and post-compulsory education research. Chair of the Society for Research into Higher Education (SRHE) 2010 Conference, Jill is an SRHE Council Member, Chair of SRHE's Research and Development Committee and Co-Convenor, BERA Post-Compulsory Education and Lifelong Learning Research SIG. Author of five books and many articles, Jill is a Fellow of the Royal Society and Fellow of the Institute for Learning, with a PhD and MA (KCL), MA (Goldsmith's), MA (Cantab), PGCE (Nottingham) and BA, PG Dip (UCT). Co-Chair, *ALT-C 2008*, Jill has 23 years' senior education management experience and is an AACE Editorial Board Member and CEDEFOP VET Leadership adviser. Jill was born in Zimbabwe, though her family originally comes from Edinburgh. Jill supported DPR by helping co-organise *DPR09: Trust* at Greenwich.

Kamila Kamińska teaches in the Instytut Pedagogiki in the Uniwersytet Wroclawski in Poland. She is working with colleagues to organise a DPR conference early in 2011 in Wroclaw, with the support of academics in educational sciences, linguistics, sociology and philosophy from the University of Wroclaw, the University of Gdans, the University of Poznan, the Wroclaw Academy of Sport, the University of Lower Silesia and the Medical Academy in Poznan, together with NGO workers, a graffiti artists' group and others.

Jerome Satterthwaite has been lead editor of the Discourse, Power, Education (DPR) book series published since 2002 by Trentham Books. He is the leader of the DPR management team and member of the editorial board of the journal *Power and Education*. Jerome has worked with the Centre for Sustainable Futures and in the Faculty of Education in the University of Plymouth, as Teacher Fellow at Leeds Metropolitan University and as Associate Tutor in the Arts Faculty of the Open University. He has postgraduate qualifications in American Literature, Education, Theology and Research Methodology and a first degree in Physics.

Ewa Sidorenko is Senior Lecturer in Education and Childhood Studies in the School of Education at the University of Greenwich. Her research interests include comparative education and cultures of learning.

Ruth Smith teaches in religious studies, philosophy, and rhetoric in the Humanities and Arts Department at Worcester Polytechnic Institute in Worcester, MA, USA. Her earlier work critically addresses modern rubrics of moral theory and the structuring of society regarding terms of autonomy, self-interest and order. Her current interests involve questions about criteria for societal membership in relation to the contended, allowable grammar of civil discourse. This direction has led to thinking about the social contract as a discourse agreement, with particular attention to Hobbes and Wittgenstein in articulating gestures of everyday life. Her articles have appeared in journals that include *Cultural Critique, Signs, Journal of Religious Ethics*, and *Rhetoric Society Quarterly.*

Sieglinde Weyringer is post-doctoral assistant at the Department of Education, University of Salzburg, Austria. Her main research areas are high abilities, moral and ethical education, democratic and citizenship education and constructivism in teaching and learning environments. She was a teacher in elementary schools for 27 years. She is the founder of various initiatives for nurturing talented and gifted students, for example *Talenteschuppen, Platon Youth Forum and ECHA-Austria (European Council of High Abilities, Austria).*

Index